The Journey to Truth Is an Experience

The Journey to Truth Is an Experience

LUIGI GIUSSANI

Translated and annotated by
John Zucchi

With the assistance of
Patrick Stevenson

McGill-Queen's University Press
Montreal & Kingston · London · Ithaca

© McGill-Queen's University Press 2006

ISBN-13: 978-0-7735-3147-5   ISBN-10: 0-7735-3147-5 (cloth)
ISBN-13: 978-0-7735-3148-2   ISBN-10: 0-7735-3148-3 (paper)

Legal deposit fourth quarter 2006
Bibliothèque nationale du Québec

Printed in Canada on acid-free paper

This book is a translation of *Il cammino al vero è un'esperienza*,
© Fraternità di Comunione e Liberazione.

McGill-Queen's University Press acknowledges the support of
the Canada Council for the Arts for our publishing program. We also
acknowledge the financial support of the Government of Canada
through the Book Publishing Industry Development Program
(BPIDP) for our publishing activities.

Library and Archives Canada Cataloguing in Publication

Giussani, Luigi
    The journey to truth is an experience / Luigi Giussani; translated and
    annotated by John Zucchi; with the assistance of Patrick Stevenson.

    Includes bibliographical references and index.
    ISBN-13: 978-0-7735-3147-5   ISBN-10: 0-7735-3147-5 (bnd)
    ISBN-13: 978-0-7735-3148-2   ISBN-10: 0-7735-3148-3 (pbk)

    1. Comunione e liberazione. I. Zucchi, John E., 1955-
    II. Stevenson, Patrick III. Title.
    BX814.C663G5913 2006   267'.182   C2006-903725-6

Typeset in Palatino 10.5/13
by Infoscan Collette, Quebec City

Contents

NOTES ON THE CHRISTIAN METHOD

Foreword

TO FIND ONESELF
AND DWELL IN CHRIST

At times life offers some momentous experiences that awaken and provoke a decisive change of direction. I remember one day in the Grand Séminaire in Montreal I noted that some of my companions did not seem to be making the same discoveries, on the spiritual plane, as I was. I was struck and disturbed by this and it led me to the Priests of Saint Sulpice, where I dedicated myself to priestly training. My discovery of something lacking in their formation was the catalyst for my vocation to train priests.

Father Luigi Giussani took the reverse path. As a young priest he taught at the Major Seminary of Milan. One day, thanks to a chance conversation with some high-school students on a train, he became aware that something was missing in the Christian experience of youth taught in Catholic institutions. He was so troubled by this that he quit his professorial duties to dedicate himself to the Christian education of young high-school students. His courageous choice was at the origin of a great ecclesial movement that has never ceased to grow and develop in Italy and in numerous other countries.

The Journey to Truth Is an Experience gathers some of the fundamental intuitions of this exceptional educator, who, like a modern-day Socrates, develops free and responsible personalities, introducing them to the total reality of human experience. He knows how to gradually recall, question, and lead his interlocutor to a free choice that culminates in the encounter with Jesus Christ at the heart of life.

That he was the object of his disciples' deep affection can be very naturally explained by the essential discovery that he provoked in them, by having them experience their own identity in Jesus Christ. Thanks to this affection, which responds to an authentic spiritual paternity, many young people and even those not so young have been able to rediscover the Church as an experience of communion that gives meaning to life.

Two questions nourish the dialogue of the members of Communion and Liberation at the "School of Community" and draw them together to educate them: "Who am I?" and "Who do you say I am?" The two go hand in hand and refer us to two analytical factors that are never neglected by the author: rational analysis and the gaze of the believer who tries to embrace all the factors of human experience, neglecting none. Whoever risks this Christian path of education knows that one must commit one's freedom if one wishes to access the depths of an experience of God that carries its own confirmation within.

Giussani's pedagogy begins from human experience and leads to a deeper level of this same experience. It helps integrate the affections of the heart and the spirit in a way that avoids rationalism and fideism, thanks to the attention paid to the "person to Person" encounter at the heart of the Christian experience. The outcome is a deep awareness of the identity of each person's "I" in Christ: this is the result of a clear-eyed and serene alliance to the ecclesial community.

The strength of this Christian path of education is the quality of experience that it facilitates and confirms, thanks to the communital verification that is an essential requirement and commits us in personal witness. "I know who I have believed in" Father Giussani might say, along with Saint Paul, thus clearly transmitting a personal conviction that becomes an extraordinary source of meaning and motivation for those who enter this fascinating experience of reality. May the reading of this book help those spirits in search of truth and those believers in search of a personal experience that may be at the same time deeply ecclesial.

Cardinal Marc Ouellet
Archbishop of Quebec and Primate of Canada

Translator's Preface

This volume is a translation of three booklets published by Luigi Giussani for the students involved in the experience to which he gave birth in 1954, *Gioventù Studentesca* (Student Youth), also known as *GS*. The name sprang from earlier Catholic youth experiences, as did its regular meetings, known as *"il raggio"* or *"the ray."* As Giussani explains in his introduction, he detected an incapacity in the Catholic world to respond to the crisis of secularism or laicism and he offered a new vision and method to live the faith, one that was rooted not in theory or discussion but in an experience. Although he was reluctant to name this new experience a movement, Giussani understood that something "different" was taking place among the young people following him and he committed to print some of his dialogues, lessons, and guidance. The booklets were published during the period of significant growth of *GS* among high-school students in Milan, in other parts of Italy, and then beyond to Brazil.

Riflessioni sopra un'esperienza (*Reflections on an Experience*) was published in late 1959, *Tracce di esperienza cristiana* (*Traces of the Christian Experience*) in late 1960, and *Appunti di metodo cristiano* (*Notes on the Christian Method*) in late 1964.

The three texts were collected in a single volume in 1972, entitled *Tracce di esperienza cristiana e appunti di metodo cristiano*, and a new edition, *Il cammino al vero è un'esperienza*, was published in 1995.

Neither edition had notes, although many biblical references were cited in parentheses in the text. I have moved all biblical citations to notes at the end of each section (which corresponds to the original booklet) and have added others that were not in the original, as well as other references. I have also inserted explanatory notes in order to give the reader context regarding names, places and particular words.

The first of the three original booklets, the *Reflections*, a work of historical value, is a methodological guide, one might say a manual, for living the Christian life in community, in this case the specific community of *GS* in the 1960s, and for this reason might seem curious to the reader. However, we have placed it at the start to maintain the original chronological order of these works. The second booklet, *Traces*, shows the path of the Christian experience, starting from the anthropological question, proceeding to the encounter with Christ, and continuing all the way to the Christian existence in service of the Kingdom of God. The second part of this volume constantly calls the reader back to a comparison of his or her experience with that of the apostles and others in the New Testament, in their relationship with Christ. The third part, *Notes on the Christian Method*, outlines the adventure of the Church, the possibility of encounter, communion, and the dimensions of mission, culture, and charity that constitute its life.

Giussani often wrote in a stilted Italian because he had such a profound sense of the philosophical weight of words and struggled to use the most adequate language to approximate Mystery. We wish to maintain at least some traces of that style in the translation, at times sacrificing style for faithfulness to the original.

John Zucchi

The Journey to Truth Is an Experience

Introduction

THE BIRTH OF AN EXPERIENCE

This volume assembles the writings that gave an initial, organically expressed form to what was being lived at the beginnings of the movement Communion and Liberation, then called *Gioventù Studentesca*, or *GS*.[1]

To re-propose them today is to re-discover the birth of an experience. These writings often originated as notes from Sunday-morning lessons given at 5 via San Antonio in Milan, Italy, the headquarters of Catholic Action in that city. They are really a "reflection on an experience" and it is not coincidental that this is the title of the first basic booklet presented here. One of the early texts passed around was Jean Guitton's *Nouvel Art de Penser* (*The New Art of Thinking*), where the author astutely observes that "a reasonable person is one who submits reason to experience." At that time, as today, it was clear that even a methodological reflection is born within a personal experience, an experience of belonging to the Christian event, which is deeply conscious, to the point of affective commitment. We felt then, exactly as we do now, that this experience was given to us to allow us to live in an existentially new way, because the way to pursue what we had seen in Scripture, in the teaching and the witness of some great teachers, appeared as something new. It was not a matter of inventing but of discovering how the tradition found new life in an experience present and appropriate to youth, from that first tiny group to so many others today – young and not so young – who have spread through fifty-nine countries, living what has affirmed itself as a method, a way, to know and love Jesus.

The discoveries and the educational concerns of these early writings, going back forty years, have developed coherently in all their successive expressions, particularly more recent ones.

Halfway through the 1950s, as I have mentioned elsewhere,[2] the common opinion was that the Church was still a solid and deeply rooted presence in Italian society, but this opinion was founded on a strength of the past, and expressed itself on one hand through mass participation in Catholic worship, and on the other – paradoxically – through a strictly political power, very much exploited from an ecclesial point of view; so much so that a large part of both ecclesial and political organisms – often the latter was the flip side of the former – showed that they were not aware of the importance of the problem of education and therefore of cultural creativity.

In those years I was a lecturer at the Seminary of Venegono,[3] teaching Dogmatic Theology in the seminary courses and Eastern-Rite Theology in the faculty. I would not have foreseen any changes but for a small episode that was to change my life and work. During a train journey to the Adriatic coast, I fell into conversation with a group of students. I found them shockingly ignorant of the nature and aim of Christian life and the Church. I then thought of dedicating myself to re-establishing a Christian witness in the school environment, where there seemed to be no Christian presence and where the anti-Catholic battle of teachers and groups with secular or laicist ideas and values was clearly advancing. I will leave to another time the historical reconstruction of what happened shortly afterwards, and what the beginning of our experience meant at the level of relationships within the ecclesial and civic communities.

As I climbed for the first time the three steps at the entrance to the *Liceo Berchet*,[4] where I had been sent to teach religion, it was clear to me, although I was aware of my limitations, that this was a matter of re-launching the announcement of Christianity as a present event of human interest and suitable for anyone who does not want to renounce the fulfillment of his or her hopes and expectations, as well as the use, without diminishment, of the gift of reason. All that was to follow, with both the élan and the imperfections inherent in every human effort, depended, and still depends, only on that first intuition.

These booklets document the reasons and the consequent methodological notations that accompanied the formation of the early student communities. The *"raggio"* (ray), the weekly meeting to which the community in each institute would invite all their companions, was the first cell of the organism. Père Maurice Cocagnac,[5] then director of the authoritative "Vie Spirituelle," on passing through Milan, said that he had seen nothing like it in all of Europe as far as the novelty of the organization and its educative effectiveness were concerned. The fundamental characteristic of the *raggio* was the comparison the youngsters were asked to draw between the theme proposed by the agenda (which would be taken from events at school, or something reported in the newspapers, or existentially important writings appropriate for their age) and their own lived experience. Thus the problems were tackled not on the basis of a theoretical or abstract dialectic but by bringing to the fore criteria and ideals already validated in experience. In this way any sentimental escape or identification of the religiosity of life with a discourse could be corrected. All this was going on while most discussions over faith, then as today, seemed to be concerned with questions "way above the clouds" (to use an expression that a Marxist teacher used to label the address of one of the greatest Catholic intellectuals of the time who was invited to one of our conventions).

Naturally, there was no lack of difficulties and misunderstandings, if not open hostility, especially on the part of those (and in those years, this meant almost the entire Catholic intelligentsia) who, doggedly maintaining the principle of the substantial separation of the religious and temporal spheres, helped to relegate faith to an ambit of abstraction, depriving it of any influence on the plane of cultural judgment and of any interest on the existential plane by reducing it to something regarding only the spiritual realm. Thus the youngsters, large numbers of whom still took part in the official events of Catholic associations, failed to find a proposal in the environments where they spent most of their day (school, factory, or office) that could show how Christian faith and life were able to answer the theoretical and existential problems that surface most dramatically in the teenage years. So participation in these associations and in the parishes tended to become more and more formal until it fell off with a speed that surprised nobody except those who did not want to see the writing on the wall. It was in those early difficult years that the fatherhood of the Church emerged in the magnanimity of people like Cardinal Montini[6] who, while admitting difficulty in understanding our methods, invited us to keep going upon seeing the first fruits.

In this context, for many the encounter with a schoolmate offering a leaflet with the agenda for the *raggio*, or inviting you to recite an hour of the office of the Liturgy, or to enjoy a holiday in the mountains, or to partake in the cultural and civic battles for freedom in education meant the rediscovery of the human value of faith; it meant a passion for verifying a Christian position regarding all of reality that was not conceived of as opposing the use of reason but as exalting it by clarifying the real structure and dynamics of openness to reality that is the ultimate nature of reason. What has every single thing (from holidays to mathematics, from falling in love to social commitment) to do with Christ? This was the question that moved us: the rediscovery, in terms of experience, of the meaning of the word "catholic."

As I have already said, the methodological development, whose early and definitive documents appear in this volume, derives from the initial decisiveness. It is not by chance that the first chapter of the first text is dedicated to "a decisive gesture"; and the decision that drove me to climb those steps was to commit myself in a no-nonsense announcement of the Christian fact, peeling away all that seemed secondary so as to reveal its essential form. I would say to the first group of youngsters: "Let us aim above all at announcing Christ, the all-embracing event in man's life and the centre of history," as John Paul II's first encyclical, *Redemptor hominis*, would clearly reaffirm. It was the essence of the Christian fact as a proposal of life. In fact we began just like that, speaking of Christ.

All this was happening at a time when the traditional meeting-places of young Catholics (parishes, youth clubs, etc.) were spending vast sums on entertainment equipment that they hoped would persuade youth to stay in touch.

Our decision to emphasize the essential led to the small and great cultural battles into which the youth of GS threw themselves generously and courageously – all this without any plans but for an immediate development of culture and affective energy. The first step dealt with freedom of education. It occurred in an ideological and ecclesial context that was insensitive, when not actually hostile, to every opposition to that type of contorted freedom of conscience, and therefore of education and cultural expression, whose grave consequences and most underhanded applications we see today. These initiatives were accompanied by the charitable activities ("caritativa"),[7] through which youngsters learned the meaning of gratuitousness as the law of existence, and missionary zeal as the superabundance of passion for the encounter they had experienced. At the same time, the desire sprang up in some of them to live a form of total dedication to Christ in the world, sowing the first seeds of what is today the *Memores Domini* association. A movement was born.

We had grasped very clearly from the start, albeit implicitly, that the Christian's only true and specific contribution to the human effort to improve one's condition in society is to bear witness to the religious position as the most completely human stance for tackling the moral, social, and political problems that one meets within social co-existence. We make this contribution above all by re-establishing ourselves as a lived Christian reality, in which the unity of the community is the first miracle pointing to Christ as the catalyst of human values and as a sure beginning of a moral journey, otherwise unthinkable with regard to purity[8] and to the infinite capacity to pick up again. An intelligence that is stirred spurs us on to repeat Peter's "Yes" to Christ's question, "Do you love me?" That "yes" generates the energy for witness and for a new morality that can be faced, like a new dawn, no matter what the circumstances; a "yes" born of sharing life with the presence of Christ, a presence gazed upon and imitated increasingly as being the only thing that corresponds to the fundamental needs of human nature, of the heart, which is the term used in the Bible to mean all of man, in his intelligence and affection. For, as time goes by, Christ's presence reveals its ultimate and fundamental dimension: the manifestation of the Father's merciful mystery, through obedience, which is the supreme virtue in which Saint Paul sums up every aspect of human experience in Christ.

Then, as today, one of the aspects that most struck the youngsters who shared our experience was its unity. We would often use the term "community" to mean the phenomenon with which Christ carries on His presence in history. Particular communities are like the gesture with which the great community of the Church reaches a person's environment. The terms "community" and "communion," understood as the animating principle, and "people," understood as the organic development of the community in all the wealth of the original contribution that Christians give to the life of the world (that "ethnic reality *sui generis*," as Paul VI called it), were not yet conceptually distinct, but their value was apparent in the gathering of those first groups in Milan and shortly afterwards throughout Italy and abroad.

The rich and lively history of forty years of the movement leaves the methodological value of these short writings unaltered. Their synthesis was derived from the need of every experience to set down the judgments and initiatives that it engenders. Their original nature derives from the fact they are not the fruit of an analysis of the social or ecclesial climate, but were formed from within the experience as it developed.

As I re-read these pages, I feel a moving gratitude at seeing a work that is being achieved, despite our limitations and our weaknesses, through the countless examples of generosity, sacrifice, and purity that many of our travelling companions have contributed, and still do, to the glory of Christ in this world; and gratitude to the Church that has decided authoritatively to welcome and confirm this experience in its journey through history.

19 October 1995

NOTES

1 "Student Youth" in English.
2 Luigi Giussani, *Le Mouvement Communion et Liberation: entretien avec Robi Ronza*. Paris: Fayard 1988, 11–13.
3 The seminary of the Archdiocese of Milan, in the town of Venegono in the city's hinterland.
4 The *Liceo Berchet* is a high-school or *lycée* in the centre of Milan. Giussani began teaching religion in this school in 1954.
5 Père Maurice Cocagnac, a French Dominican friar, theologian, and composer of religious music, was born in 1924.

6 Giovanni Battista Montini (1897–1978) was Archbishop of Milan from 1954 until his election as Pope Paul VI in 1963.

7 As the following chapters will clearly show, the term "caritativa" has a much more pregnant meaning than "charitable activity." It refers to the dedication of one's free time to sharing with others, perhaps less fortunate than oneself, the experience of the Christian life encountered. As the text explains, the usefulness of this activity is tied to its educational value for those involved, rather than to its effectiveness in helping those in need.

8 Here Giussani refers to "purità" and not "purezza," that is, purity in the profound moral sense of authenticity.

Gioventù Studentesca
or Student Youth

Reflections on an Experience

1 Methodological Instructions on the Christian Proposal

DECISIVENESS AS A GESTURE

1 The first condition for reaching anyone is a clear definition of what we hope to achieve.

2 We must avoid presenting ourselves, no matter what the milieu, in a way that appears indecisive. While we might be tempted to weaken our proposal because we fear that our ideas will conflict with the current mentality, making others ill-disposed towards us and creating insurmountable misunderstandings and distancing, to do so can lead us to illusion and ambiguity. We may be tempted to look for ways to accommodate and camouflage our ideas, which may perhaps be done astutely, but this can easily lead to inescapable compromises.

3 We must not forget that this "current mentality" exists not only outside ourselves; it permeates us to the core, so that indecisiveness in confronting it could destroy us.

4 Honesty demands that at some point we confront serious problems, not only those that require dealing with our own conscience but also in dialogue with others.

5 That is why we need the strength to place ourselves "in opposition," which is what Christ asked of us if we wish to enter the Kingdom: "He who will have been ashamed of me before others, so shall I also be ashamed of him before my Father."[1]

6 Strength, that is, *courage*, (*virtus* in Latin): ultimately, what we need is some of that virtue with which Matthew, Zacchaeus, and Mary Magdalene affirmed their Christian discovery in their particular circumstances.

Or, if you will, we need to renew Stephen's testimony before the Sanhedrin: to flout the common opinion in order to follow Jesus.

CLEAR COMMUNICATION

1 It is through us that Christ proposes himself to men and women. Our attitude and words constitute the proposal through which others can know him.

Our communication must therefore be clear, that is simple, if it is to be addressed to *everyone*.

2 Simplicity has less to do with the way we say something – only some people are able to do this well – than with avoiding complicated, extraneous matters. It has to do with keeping to the essential.

3 Even Christ's proposal in the beginning was simple and essential: in fact He proposed that only specific truths (dogmas), sacramental gestures, and authority in the community were compulsory, thus making it clear that the Church is extremely careful about the elements it considers to be compulsory.

4 It is easy to understand the wisdom of the behaviour of Christ and the Church. Someone with such simplicity can be flexible enough to address any individual. Only by striving for the essential can we reach our goal without undue stress.

Accurate identification of the essential factors of existence leads us to:
– strongly affirm their value and thus to adhere to them resolutely;
– have a broad understanding of all the positions that we meet, which enables us to value and embrace an infinite variety of such positions.

5 A point to consider: simple does not mean "generic." It means *accuracy regarding the substantive factors and freedom regarding any interpretation and application.*

Jesus said: "Go forth through the entire world and preach to all the peoples." Each person is responsible for a specific task ("go forth and preach") but is free to choose how to achieve his or her particular vocation.

The conditions for simplicity are freedom, action, and concreteness.

Freedom

1 The Christian calling is addressed to each particular individual and, more specifically, to his or her freedom.

2 When God turns to man to ask something of him, the Bible describes the dialogue with sublime simplicity. God calls by name, which is the sign of the person as a unique and free individual; and the person's adherence is free and unique: *"here I am!"*

In Christianity, the only thing that matters is *the value of the person*, because everything else depends on this; and the value of the person is measured by that free adherence.

This is most evident in the historical figures of Abraham and Christ. Perhaps the most understandable and clearest moment for us is the figure of the Blessed Virgin. "Ave Maria – Fiat": In the impenetrable *free* intimacy of this gesture of offering and acceptance lies the cornerstone of God's mysterious encounter with the human person.

3 Our proposal must be exclusively an echo of that "Voice that calls each by name."

Therefore its objective must be to reach out *directly to the freedom* of those to whom it is addressed. We must perseveringly elicit their *awareness* and provoke their *initiative*.

Ignorance and passivity are limits to freedom. Woe that we should count on them to "seize" and "hold on" to people! Adherence to Christianity, inasmuch as it is purely mechanical, has no value. Thus, we must question any purely traditional attachment or sudden enthusiasm. Freedom's proper setting is enlightened and conscious conviction.

4 If we wish to solicit another's freedom genuinely then we must *act freely*. Only one's own commitment can reach another person. The Christian proposal can only be offered to another seriously. The communication of Christianity is thus the encounter of two freedoms, *the reference of one person to another*.

Thus, it is love: "He has elected us in Him … for love."[2]

Any generic attitude is useless: it is either negligence or presumption.

5 We have said that to address the freedom of the other means to provoke a conscious initiative. Such an initiative can have *many nuances*; that is, the answer can be given in a great variety of ways and at many levels.

To choose people based on the *expectancy of particular levels of response* would be to forget the essential reference to pure freedom. Even pure and simple presence can constitute the initiative of a true response.

Action

1 After a person has heard the proposal, has been given the choice of accepting it or not, and has had his or her freedom solicited, he or she faces the problem of continuing to adhere to the calling as in the beginning. If I understand that something is right, how can I continue to desire it? The answer is by committing myself, by acting, by "building up" the reality that I see as right. The initial participation must become a continuous constructiveness. To commit oneself to reality means to live it, and only if something is alive can it be continuous.

2 The means of continuity therefore is "to take action." But there are two conditions:

– "Taking action" *must not have pre-imposed limits*. We cannot say: "I'll try a number of times, and then if I am unable and I don't like it, that's it!"

Such an attitude reveals at its origins a subtle lack of love for the Truth as well as a subtle presumption or attachment to oneself.

– *Any gesture* (any "doing") engages the entire person, so that even a minimal activity, accepted for the Ideal, makes a valid contribution to the person's growth.

Often we hold back from committing ourselves because we feel we are incapable of a higher level of accomplishment. We abandon everything because the peak seems almost unattainable or simply because what others do seems impossible for us. Nothing is more irrational than to be intimidated by something good. Let each one do what he or she can. No matter what the circumstances, even the worst, one is not excused from trying again and again, persistently. Vita non facit saltus ("life does not take leaps and bounds"), so we cannot hope to reach the summit immediately; we need the patience to grow, a patience as long as the Lord's – which is to say, the length of our entire life.

3 Any person's initiative always springs from within himself or herself. Any action flows only from our will. Others can push us or call us towards a commitment, but there is a point at which only our free will is engaged. This is true for any moment or level of our development, so that our action is a continuous *creation of our freedom*.

4 It is also true, however, that normally if there is to be continuity after the initial commitment, the calling must persist. Hence begins the *educational relationship* (with a parent, teacher, spiritual director, friends ...).

The educative dialogue must not limit itself to an exchange of ideas or words (lessons, sermons, warnings, admonitions), for ideas remain abstract until one lives them: unless you live them, you do not feel that they are part of you. The abstract can be a momentary fascination that, however, does not become a vital fluid. Ideas, even if sublime and well expressed, do not educate unless they are seized within a lived experience. Thus the educational relationship is that of an *experience lived together*; the educative dialogue must be understood as a *gesture in common*.

5 One of our most common excuses for renouncing our original commitment is disgust with the attitude of those very persons or surroundings that first solicited the calling in us.

The truer a person, the more he or she must know how to *distinguish* the value of each proposal from its expression or the situations to which it is linked. Those who want to grow up must deny themselves irrational positions of revolt against a truth simply because the one who calls them to that truth translates it in an unsuitable way or lives it inconsistently.

Concreteness

1 When Saint Jerome wrote about God's "condescension" towards us he meant to emphasize how Christ made himself man to communicate with us; that is, He made Himself one with us. He did not wait for us to change, that we might be less sinful; instead He redeemed us in our most human condition. "It was He who loved us first,"[3] says Saint Paul. This initiative of His in

love is repeated in time and space. "No one comes unto me unless the Father leads him. Ask the Lord of the harvest that he might send labourers to his harvest."[4]

2 The charity of our calling must carefully consider the situation of others.

Such a consideration must never discourage us because every human reality is always receptive to the Word.

It is so easy to avoid considering reality because it is not all we hoped for; so to approach it implies a greater commitment and toil. We easily accuse reality of not matching our comforting dreams, perhaps even as we change the rules of the game, and consequently take on the attitude of a victim or proclaim ourselves powerless before circumstances.

On the other hand, the only way to consider the individual according to what he or she truly is, without preconceptions, is by carefully taking into account his or her historical situation. To understand someone we must place ourselves at that person's level.

3 Each person's concrete situation is defined:

a. by his or her *psychological situation*: For one who proposes the call this implies a very sensitive openness towards the interior situation of the other. The type of intelligence, level of knowledge, temperament, strength of will, state of health, tribulations undergone – everything helps to determine a soul's position.

b. by the environment: It is necessary to consider the milieu, which decisively influences a person's existence at a particular moment.

Our proposal cannot reach another's awareness directly. It has to penetrate a mentality, which is like a wrapping, if it is to reach the genuine "I." This mentality is like a superstructure that is to a great extent constructed by the environment. Behind this lies the nature, the psychic constitution of the person, and the environment's exasperating influence through very modern invasive means such as propaganda, school, or television. It would be vain for us to claim that we can resist or neutralize this influence if we do not succeed in reaching the person where he or she is most influenced, that is, in his or her milieu.

4 Up until a certain age the family environment prevails for youth, but later, in a period often characterized by a certain resentment towards their early surroundings, they are totally open to what is new. Their early esteem for the family setting is redirected

to the student milieu, often unawares. This is where the proposal must be offered. By student environment we mean not only the four walls of the building but also everything that is born of it: companionship, leisure time, reading, and attitudes.

Today's schools typically present ideas, experiences, and persons confusingly and indiscriminately to young people. This leads to an unstructured melange of contacts and relationships, and thus to dispersion and dissociation.

Our appeal must consider these factors very seriously. On the one hand, we need a full understanding and openness towards everything that enhances the positive, thus facilitating the individual's renewal through trust in him- or herself and in us. On the other, the Christian proposal must create and express a concrete and complete approach that is able to provide a suitable explanation for every problem that the student encounters.

5 This concrete approach can be created by educating the individual within a *personal experience*; that is, by getting him or her into the habit of comparing everything that he or she meets with a personal criterion. This does not mean an arbitrary or personal opinion, but an objective measure, independent of us insofar as it is an Other's idea, the will of God the Creator and Redeemer. However, that measure becomes immanent and personal insofar as one lives it. Christ promised the Samaritan woman that she would have such a claim to His gushing Water (that is, His Life and His Criterion) that she would no longer need to draw upon other sources.

In conclusion, the calling is a response to *everything*. That is its ultimate characteristic, because it is true. This "everything" finds its broadest expression, albeit contingent, in one's environment. That is where one discovers the calling and experiences it as the only complete response.

COMPLETE IN ITS DIMENSIONS

1 *The level of openness towards all of reality that a human gesture accomplishes is called a "dimension."* It allows us to glimpse an ultimate meaning in any endeavour. Dimensions thus represent the most important aspects of a gesture: those that measure (see "dimetior" Latin) the value of a gesture; and those that carry out all of its potential.

2 The same gesture can be lived in many different ways from the point of view of dimensions. Its original thrust can develop in all the directions that it should or it can be interrupted at a certain point, or it can achieve only some of its possibilities, forgetting or even denying the others.

3 To complete a gesture, *all of its fundamental dimensions*, those that define its true visage precisely and faithfully, must be realized.

4 To obscure or neglect any dimension of the gesture would be to make a mask, that is, an illusion or lie, of its visage.

The completeness of a gesture's dimensions is a matter not only of richness or fullness but of life or death for the gesture itself, because without at least the implicit structure of all its fundamental dimensions, the gesture is not only insignificant but also lacking in truth, contradictory in its nature, *unjust*.

5 A gesture's natural dimensions are profoundly tied one to the other. Thus the more intensely we live one of them the more open we are to living the others.

The dimensions of the Christian calling are culture, charity, and catholicity.

CULTURE

1 Culture must be able to offer us the meaning of all things. A truly cultured person is one who understands the *link* that binds one thing to another and all things to each other. Thus culture cannot be a question of having notions, because even notions that have been derived from the studies of thousands of individuals could not offer a single word to resolve the great question regarding the relationship that binds the human person to all things, that is, the meaning of his or her existence.

2 For this reason, the origin of all things, the ultimate meaning of everything, was revealed to us. "The Word became flesh" means that the Rationality that saves the universe from the absurd is not an abstract idea or a mechanism but a *person*: Jesus Christ. If one gives a meaning to the universe and sets aside Jesus Christ, its ultimate explanation, then only the absurd exists.

3 Thus the Christian call proposes itself as that which satisfies the need to comprehend reality completely, that for which the entire human conscience quivers ("I am the way, the truth, the life"[5]).

4 However, in Christianity, culture must never submit to the temptation to dissociate reason from the rest of what is human, precisely because of this identification of the ultimate explanation with the real person. Only Christianity affirms the decisive equality of the terms "man" and "cultured."

5 If the person of Christ gives a meaning to each person and to all things, then nothing in the world or in our life can live on its own and avoid being bound invincibly to Him. Thus the true cultural, Christian dimension finds expression in the *comparison* between the truth of His person and our life in all of its implications.

6 The term culture has always been strongly linked to the term *civilization*. Civilization is the full translation of a culture into the totality of human life. The birth of a Christian culture envisages and, in a certain way, already realizes a new civilization.

Charity

1 The first gesture in the history of reality consisted of a *communication* by God. He made Himself one with us. In a certain sense God shared in our nothingness: "I loved you with an eternal love; thus I attracted you to me, having compassion for your nothingness."[6] This was creation, the fundamental mystery of being, and thus the fundamental stumbling block for those proud persons who would claim to understand everything through the systematic measures or narrow evidence of reason.

But God went far beyond this with this mysterious gesture of communication. In the Incarnation of His Word, God places Himself with us in His personal reality. Christ is the gesture with which God clarifies and "takes up again" all of his creation.

And even more, God wanted this gesture to endure throughout history. The Church is Christ, present and hidden. The Church is God, who continues to place himself with us (Emmanuel – God among us). The Church is Christ, who continues to share in our life, "until the end of time."[7]

Creation, Incarnation, Church: together these are the fundamental revelations of God, that is, of Being, who, as we see in the Mystery of the Trinity, is Life as love.

2 Of course, our life, which participates in that Infinite Life, can only be truly developed by applying that mysterious method.

Here then lies the simple and direct route to developing our being, the fundamental educative norm for fulfilling our personality: to share our lives; to share divine reality and common reality as it reveals itself to us or rises up in our path; to share our lives (convivere) in order to live. "Good Master, what must I do in order to have eternal life? ... Love your neighbour as yourself."[8]

It is *charity: abandonment of oneself to God*. He takes the initiative to offer Himself to me, either directly or through human faces, filling the solitude of my nothingness. Thus charity is the paradox of my existence, in which is reflected the Mystery of the Existence of the One and Triune God: to be myself I must give myself to others. For my personality to have substance, I must lose myself in the reality of others. To live I must die. "He who seeks himself will lose himself; he who loses himself will find himself."[9] The Christian poet, Paul Claudel, reiterates this phrase in *L'Annonce faite à Marie* (*The Tidings Brought to Mary*): "Is the object of life only to live? ... It is not to live but to die ... and to give all that we have, laughing. There is joy, there is freedom, there is grace, there is eternal youth."[10]

3 We must discover, grasp, understand, and assimilate this supreme directive. *If it is present at least as a principle or concern*, then we are Christians.

Otherwise, we can do many things, but their pedagogical fruitfulness will not have a Christian measure. We may be dealing with intelligent asceticism or sacrificial, generous and philanthropic service, but it will not have the deep dimensions of the Christian gesture. This is the disconcerting surprise that we experience upon reading the thirteenth chapter of the First Letter to the Corinthians, where Saint Paul says that one can even die for others and not have love, and thus be worth nothing; that is, when we sacrifice ourselves to affirm our own ideas or to follow a feeling, and not out of devotion to the Being who reaches out to us; when we share our things, perhaps even our lives, without truly sharing ourselves; when we rid ourselves of everything without losing ourselves.

4 One final concrete observation: Human beings are imperfect and strive to find something that fulfills them; this makes us understand that existence is characterized by a permanent state of want, poverty, and need.

Therefore, to share with others will be translated practically into *sharing as much as possible in their needs* – spiritual, moral, cultural, and, yes, material needs – being aware of, understanding, and taking them upon our shoulders. And since material needs are the most immediately evident and most easily addressed, attention to sharing them is an excellent education for a deeper and more total charity that touches the value of the person as such (in this sense, Scripture praises almsgiving.)

Catholicity: The Missionary Dimension

1 In the twelfth chapter of Genesis, Abraham's vocation is entirely formulated in this limitless space: "Abandon your land … and go where I shall tell you." And further on: "You will be the head of all the peoples of the earth."[11] Boundless space and all of humanity are the dimensions of the great revelation to the Jewish people.

We also find this universal dimension when God says to Adam: "Multiply and fill all the earth."[12] *That is, universality is the condition of freedom in action.*

2 Freedom's very nature inevitably makes us experience a limit as something suffocating. Our freedom can limit the ambit of our sharing, but this is to deny ourselves. It is a sin (that is a "defect," which in its Latin origins means to fail). We are reminded of our Lord's saying: "He who sins contradicts himself."[13] When we limit our own openness to sharing our lives [convivenza] we seek to impose our own measure on the profound law of being, we confuse love with calculation, and sharing with an attempt to dominate others.

3 The endpoints of Christ's call are the extreme ends of the earth, right to the end of the world (see the conclusion of Saint Matthew's Gospel).

And Saint Paul's announcement seems natural to our soul's thirst: "Everything is yours, as you belong to Christ."

We must share our lives [convivere] with everyone, share in everyone's life. *Charity is a law without frontiers, it is universal: catholic.*

Under this law, to measure and delimit would be the same as cutting off the law itself: to impose a limit on it is not to limit but to abrogate it.

4 It is necessary to meditate on the fact that the Christian call is above all the conquest of the world in the evangelical sense: the Kingdom of God. To have a sense of the Kingdom means to have *the missionary sense*. We must live for the universe, for all of humanity. As Pius XII stated, "the universal perspectives of the Church are the normal directives of the Christian's life."

5 The more we love this universal sense the more we are capable of *faithfulness to the particular* (prayer, purity, duties, etc.). We no longer sense this faithfulness as something strict or repressive but as it truly is, freedom. Only with this ideal do we observe the greatest commandments and perform the most humble services.

6 Whoever works without this ideal can be doggedly honest, richly ascetic, perhaps even heroic, but cannot be a true *Christian*.

7 The most intimate education in this dimension is imparted by the Liturgy, which makes us say ageless words expressing an awareness as vast as the universe, with the permanence of history.

COMMUNITAL IN FULFILLMENT

1 "Woe to the man who is alone," says the Bible. The warning is also perfectly applicable to the person who must communicate the Christian proposal. An effort to propose a Christian reality that remains individualistic and avoids a systematic referral to the community would not be a *certain effort*, no matter how intelligent, giving, and active.

2 Such an effort may express a presumption or indolence. It would be a case of a *fictitious* witness, who would simply set out not to propose the Christian reality but to affirm a limited way of seeing things, a particular taste, an imprudent feeling, or merely personal convenience.

3 The individualist attitude constitutes, without doubt, a *precarious* situation, because an individual cannot continue to serve ideals on his or her own in the long run: individuals are too weak, on the inside; and the "world" on the outside, or the environment that they face, is too strong.

The transcendence of divine ideals always gives the person who desires involvement a feeling of risk, a temptation towards unreasonable fear and uncertainty. Psychologically, the energy of freedom cannot easily prevail unless it depends on community. The communital life is like the soil in which the plant of freedom can yield ripe fruits.

4 In any case, an individualistic attitude would be contrary to what Christ wanted from His disciples. The seventeenth chapter of Saint John binds the validity of the Christian tidings, as we have already considered, to the visible manifestation of unity among its followers, and thus to the effectiveness of the community as such. And, even before this, we read: "If two or three are gathered in my name, my Father will help them, because I am with them,"[14] where Jesus binds the completeness of the religious relationship to the communital aspect.

Historically, there are no Christian beginnings where there is no acute communital need.

Let us now look at the factors of community: personal adherence, functionality (to be part of a whole), authority, and visible unity.

Personal Adherence

1 Our duty is to make ours all those things with which God lavishes His generous and deep love upon us. This is precisely how our personality develops, and this is called "work."

2 This is all the more so when we are dealing with live and spiritual beings. We are called to discover their presence, to accept their person, to make their reality a part of ours; in a word, we are called to "share" in their existence and ours, to "share our life" (*convivere*) with them. This is the "work" through which our personality becomes completely mature. It is called love.

3 The Lord allows me to find myself together with and near to others. I could live by trying to keep as far apart as possible from them or by using them according to the interest and the pleasure that they represent for me, as something to exploit, or else I could live with open antagonism and aversion towards them.

In all of these cases the presence of others is an *extraneous condition to my freedom*, to my I, and thus a limit to my expression, something on which I depend and to which I am bound, or clash with.

To share my life (convivenza) with others in these cases is something external for me, more or less imposed. It becomes a defensive or offensive slyness, walking a tightrope in order to live, a great struggle for "justice."

To share my life with others in this way becomes a *collectivity*.

4 Instead, the emergence of these people by my side, those who surround me and whom I meet, are that aspect of the Creator's will that involves the greatest commitment. Thus, I must *accept* these people. By accepting them, they become mine, part of me, become me: "love thy neighbour as thyself."

It is precisely in this manner that *community* is born, as the continuous outcome of this initiative of acceptance on my part; of tireless commitment to the presence of others, to the surprising and mysterious sign of the Other, just as is my presence to myself.

Sharing my life with others then is something that springs from within me, a gesture that expresses me, a gift of myself, a *relationship of love*.

5 Thus the community is far from a limit to the personality.

In a structurally dependent being, as is the human person, *freedom always begins specifically as acceptance*. The more one knows how to accept, the more active one becomes.

Christ would draw the comparison between the vine and the branches – the only life that feeds many lives. We can apply this comparison to every true community: the life that keeps everyone together is *the power of my freedom that opens itself* and gives itself to others.

The greatness of human freedom is such that it will not rest if not in a community of *all*, a "catholic" community.

6 One thing best demonstrates how much the community affirms the freedom of the person: it is realized even if others do not acknowledge me, even if they refuse me. *If I want them, if I accept them* nonetheless, then there is a more conscious, vigorous, and thus ever truer communion with them.

For this reason, no sign of personal greatness is more sublime than *forgiveness*. Freedom seizes in love even one who hates; not even the most dogged enemy can elude my love, and thus my freedom seizes him and dominates him much more deeply than he can violate and conquer me.

"Forgive them Father"[15]: abandoned by everyone, Christ created the universal community.

7 Here is an important observation: to be in community is not an exterior "getting along," a simple convergence from the outside. To be in community is *an interior dimension, at the origin of each action*.

To be communital, a gesture must be *conceived* in unison with the community and not aimed only at a common outcome.

Functionality ("to be in service of" or "to be part of a whole")

1 Life's supreme characteristic is unity. The greater a life, the deeper and more pervasive its unity; but life wonderfully and strangely expresses this unity through evident differentiation, through unmistakable distinctions: they are called *functions*.

Animal life expresses itself through such functions as sight, memory, or digestion, for example. From a biological point of view the unitary life that expresses itself in functions is called the "organism." Even in the spiritual life one can speak of organisms, naturally by analogy, by comparison.

2 Functions are aspects of life as it expresses itself. All functions translate the indivisible unity of life into action so that their diversity does not destroy unity but shows its density and richness.

The greater a life, the more it is differentiated. In amoeba, for example, functionality is at a minimum, whereas in the human body it is very highly developed. The life of the spirit has entirely unlimited functionality; every idea, for example, is a true "function."

3 This is understandable when we reflect that "function" is the *possibility of relationship that a determined life* has with the rest of reality, *with all the rest of reality.*

Thus, the more intense, powerful, and noble a life, the more it develops contacts, forms relationships, and thus multiplies its functionality, highlighting its capacity to insert itself into reality and assert itself in the world.

4 All of this is truest for the phenomenon of community. The community is a life; it is like a true organism, so much so that its components are often called *members*, that is, functional *organs*.

The community is made up of persons, each of whom has a particular temperament and particular capacities. Some will be more fit for one task, others for other tasks, so that each is like a true function of the one life of the community.

5 The various tasks of the community are born of the diverse innate talents of its members. They originate in the variety of "vocations" among the community's components.

6 Persons are like *organs of the relationship between the community and its environment.*

And it is specifically through this relationship that the community establishes and enriches itself.

Individuals act in the service of the community's integration into the world; thus they allow the community to fulfill and develop itself and to express its true vibrancy.

7 Thus a community is all the more alive the more its members are capable of varied and multiple functions.

8 However, even a communital life is all the stronger the more it is *specifically and intensely hierarchical in its functions* and tasks. In such tasks the various forces, otherwise dissipated, are channelled to become more organized and more useful to all.

9 To accept this diversity of tasks; to look for our own limits carefully, serenely, and willingly; to acknowledge sincerely in someone else a capacity superior to our own; to collaborate with generously and to respect deeply everyone who has a function – all of this *measures one's spirit of community.*

Authority

1 Among the various tasks carried out by the members of a community, the most meaningful is giving consistency to the community and expressing it in its totality, that is, in its inspiring principle and in its reality: *the unifying function of the community.* That is the task of authority.

Authority is thus the expressive sign of unity, but above all it is the founding and responsible function of all the life of the community.

2 This is a triple function:
– to solicit people's initiative to form a community (*the function of calling* others);
– to preserve the features of the community, defining it clearly within its limits (*the function of the ultimate point of reference*);
– to develop the community, establishing it ever more firmly in reality (*the function of education*).

3 Naturally, the community's guide should be the person most aware of the ideals of the group and most capable of living and communicating them. Thus authority, rather than being a right, *should be a fact, the fact of an exceptional communital spirit.*

But once authority has been established, love of the community demands adherence to that authority no matter who its embodiment may be.

The individual member of the community cannot have the right to ignore that authority, claiming that the authority is inadequate.

An authority can be removed only by the rule that has established that authority. Thus, for example, in a democracy the authority can be changed by the will of the majority, according to the conventions created by the state.

4 We have already seen that the community is the expression of our freedom. Because authority epitomizes and represents the community in its total unity, to accept authority is not a limitation but the summit of our personality's expression.

We abandon ourselves to authority, that is, we love others as ourselves above all, in *obedience*. "Why torment ourselves so much when it is so simple to obey?" says Anne Vercors in *L'Annonce faite à Marie* (*The Tidings Brought to Mary*).[16]

5 The rule of *following*: this is the ultimate dynamic of any method of education. It cannot be eliminated. To advance towards the fullness of our personality is only truly possible in the concrete gesture of leaving behind our own limits to adhere passionately to the hypothesis of total meaning that authority implies. Education without authority is impossible by nature, in that it leaves the person to be educated *alone* in the struggle to overcome his or her limitations. An education without authority is impossible in any case, even practically speaking, in that it is impossible that our humanity be attracted by nothing else but itself. The Christian community values and takes to the limit the natural rule of education, of following an authority.

Yet even this acceptance can reveal the profoundly different commitment that the individual lives in the community. One might be aware of authority and consider it a factor external to oneself, often only to be judged and criticized. This is a passive, uncommitted attitude. Instead, one must *make oneself present to authority*: that is, offer oneself actively to it, in an untiring dialogue of collaboration, like Christ's dialogue with the Father.

6 If the community is my person in its greater reality and thus more alive and free, authority must be loved as the most expressive part of myself. To accept authority so readily is the richest way to *share*, the truest charity.

Visible Unity

1 The law of life is charity, but it is clear that sharing the existence of others unites me to them, generates a real unity of life with them. The Son placed a seal on the Mystery of His total communion, of His perfect "participation" in the Father – the assertion that "The Father and I are one thing only."[17]

The *strength of unity is the measure of the power of a life*, just as dissociation and dispersion are the measure of death. Thus Christ, in His final testament, reminds His disciples of unity as the sign of true charity, and defines the loving commerce of life between God and His people with the sublime words: "You in me, and I in them, may they be consumed in unity."[18]

2 Just as sharing is not genuine if it is not structurally open to the universe, neither *does a true sense of the universal exist if it is not a passion for unity*. The more we communicate an activity the more deeply do we sense the need for unity. The more self-aware a personality the more it opens up to the world and the more intense its experience of unity becomes. *The experience of the universal and the particular coincide.*

The sense of unity is the unremitting lived need to understand all things in their relationship with all other things. This is the sign of a mature awareness, a cultivated person, a genius.

3 Let us consider, then, that only the dimension of unity demonstrates the presence of true charity and of universality. The cry of Jacopone da Todi, "love, love cries the entire world, love, love, all things together acclaim," is born of the same experience as *The Imitation of Christ*: "From the single Word everything, and all things say one, and this is the principle which also speaks in you."

4 It is necessary, however, to note that the unity of Christ is not only unity of spirit and conscience. What is not *visibly expressed* is not true unity.

What we translate into the tangible and visible truly conforms to nature, to our complex balance of flesh and spirit. This is the very concrete position of Catholic unity before the Protestant claim of interior unity.

Thus *the mature expression of Christian sharing is unity, including the tangible and visible*. That was the expression of Christ's final torment in His prayer to the Father, when He indicated that the decisive testimony of His friends consisted of such a tangible and visible unity.

5 The love of unity, which is also tangible and visible, is the criterion for assessing whether we love the Ideal more than a preconceived vision, our standing in the community, or ourselves.

One must even accept to die for unity.

2 The Effort to Achieve Something Practical: *Gioventù Studentesca*

An example in practice: *Gioventù Studentesca* (Student Youth or *GS*)
– The starting point of *GS*: decisiveness
– The reality of *GS*: the *raggio* (the "ray")
The *raggio* is built on: freedom, action, concreteness
– The development of the *GS* experience
A path for its development: conquest of culture, charitable activity, missionary activity, perceivable unity; the "centre" of *GS*
– The goal: a new environment

THE STARTING POINT: DECISIVENESS

1 *GS*'s starting point is the existence of some *persons* in a given student environment who have an active and serious perception of the Christian reality.

2 *Active*: that is to say, having a sensitivity that motivates them and generates the need for contacts and communication; that produces energy.

This is quite different from a shy reserve, a detached unease, or a stubborn indifference.

Serious: that is to say, engaging the essential factors of one's own personality, inquisitive intelligence, and moral strength; thus one is beyond every rhetoric and preconceived opinion.

Some may sense Christian reality more as a problem of truth; others as a question regarding rightness and goodness.

The first case is often prevalent in the early high-school years, at least in boys, and this is why a serious attitude towards Christianity will often manifest itself as a desire and effort to be loyal to the truth.

3 To start off in such a way you do not have to consider yourself a saint or morally better than others.

The Samaritan woman drew the people of her town to Jesus.

4 To start off you don't need organizational skills or other particular talents.

GS is not proposed as an organization for trips, competitions, exhibitions, etc. It is not a student club, nor is it groups of friends who get together because they like each other or for popular recreational activities.

GS proposes itself *exclusively* as a reminder of the Christian fact.

5 To have a starting point for GS there must be, in every town, school, or class, a person who becomes involved in a relationship with his or her companions over an aspect of Christianity that he or she finds of interest and communicates to them, even if it is only out of concern about a problem.

That person can be *anyone*, even a shy girl or a not particularly bright boy: anyone who is *decisive in what he or she is doing.*

THE REALITY OF *GS*:
THE *RAGGIO* OR "RAY"

Freedom

1 Awareness is the first condition for freedom.

GS starts off as an interior reminder. When you listen to a companion or a priest, you realize that you need to clarify your Christianity, for or against; you realize that you need to confront yourself personally with the Christian reality that you were born into.

So GS arises as *personal awareness of the Christian proposal.*

2 But freedom is measured by *consonance with your conscience.* So it is commitment.

The reality of *GS* is measured exclusively by the commitment of its members: this commitment may at first be less than complete, but eventually it must become concrete.

GS is not a reality that some organize and others follow, as if drawn along: it is only present where someone undertakes a *personal initiative.*

3 Anything human – and therefore the phenomenon of personal initiative – if it is to last, needs *time, space, and others.* Our freedom before the Christian call begins when we devote time to Christianity, and it begins to achieve something when it accepts community with others.

Those who *set aside time to work together for the Christian Ideal* give *GS* its first formation.

We need to note that this implies an awareness of one's own limitations, a basic capacity to sacrifice oneself and one's individualism, to overcome total trust in oneself, one's self-sufficiency and pride.

This is how the *raggio* is born.

The *raggio* is the minimum reference time and space, the first physical formulation of *GS.*

Simply being present at the *raggio* is only a start, but it is still a true participation in *GS.*

4 The proposal must be aimed at absolutely *everyone.*

That "everyone" is selected by their participation – or not – in the *raggio.*

So *GS* is always *the outcome of this choice: it is not decided by the one who calls, but by the freedom of those who are listening.*

Action

1 Once it has begun, *how* is the *raggio* carried out? How is that presence, initiative, commitment developed? In practice all this corresponds with the question of how to *live* the Christian proposal once you have heard it, since only by living something can you go on believing, and therefore understanding and feeling it.

The *raggio* must be the tangible locus of this life.

2 Relationships between persons are lived through signs, which are gestures: words are only one form of gesture, albeit an important one. Through gestures a person expresses and communicates; in others words, becomes engaged with others.

This personal communication through gestures is called dialogue. The *raggio* is carried out as a dialogue.

3 Obviously this dialogue is far from a rationalist notion of dialectic that would conceive of dialogue as a more or less lucid clash of ideas and mentalities.

Our dialogue is the mutual communication of ourselves through the signs of words, gesture, and attitudes: the emphasis is not on ideas, but on the person as such, on freedom. Our dialogue is life, and ideas are one expression of this life.

Describing the Mystery of God made man, the Scripture says, "cum hominibus conversatus est" ("He dialogued with man").[1] Dialogue is communicating one's own personal life to other personal lives; dialogue is sharing the existence of others in one's own existence; it is a gift of self.

4 In a dialogue you give what you have. So the more you give the more you have a personality, the more mature you are.

5 *The first sign* of maturity is awareness and consciousness of your own being. The more you are aware of your own human experience, the more mature you are. Thus maturity is above all awareness of the reason for your own living.

This *measures* the first possibility you have to give, to enter into dialogue.

Let us emphasise some levels of this consciousness.

a. *Listening*

What is the most primitive aspect of that maturity? The beginning of maturity is an awareness of *not having* something, of our own limitations, of what we lack. So the first way to dialogue at the *raggio* is to know how to listen. Listening is the first gesture through which you give yourself to others and share your life. Listening is the first gesture that fills the presence at the *raggio* with life.

b. *Preparing oneself*

However, besides not having something, we *do have* something. Everyone has something to give. From this point of view maturity is demonstrated by generosity in preparing oneself for the *raggio*. If you do not do so, your personality will not emerge. To be helped in this you must first reflect on and become aware of what you have.

A practical technique to help us prepare is to distribute an agenda, if possible at the beginning of the week. It may list the problems to consider at the next meeting, and guidelines for tackling them. The more we reflect on the theme of the *raggio* in preparatory meditations during the week, the more will it become a dialogue. The *raggio* should come to be an expression and communication of a whole week's work; then it becomes a barometer of how the commitment has been lived.

We should choose basic arguments for the agenda, not so much issues that lead to intellectual clashes, or subtle explanations, or exegesis of texts from the Gospels or Saint Paul. We should choose arguments that touch on life; then it will be easier to communicate.

GS is not the place where all is made clear: *GS* aims to help students to better understand themselves. To understand yourself you do not need to solve all your problems at once. Understanding yourself means taking up your own position before reality, living the fundamental law that is openness and charity.

If you do this, then all will become clear. Erudite and subtle discussion leaves us empty, except for a few particular temperaments.

c. *Speaking*

To the extent to which you become aware of what you are living you can *speak of* it.

That dialogue is charity, and therefore an education in sharing our lives, as is revealed by the two-fold difficulty that it implies. First, there is the often unbearable effort to overcome that fear or reserve or diffidence or skepticism that prevents you from speaking out, which reveals a range of symptoms: introversion, self-attachment, uneducated conceit. You genuinely experience how difficult it is to break something down, to have to break down an invisible locked door. Many people can go to the *raggio* for months, or even years, with the desire to overcome this reserve, but each time can only manage to listen. All the same this effort is already an education in openness: sooner or later their faithfulness will bear fruit.

Second, there is the difficulty of holding back, controlling what you say (this seems to be the opposite of the first difficulty); not only to avoid the gauche error of saying too much, but to prevent us making the more subtle mistake of being concerned only with speaking and not with listening and thus understanding what others have in mind or how they feel. In other words, we have to put our interior brakes on. This is a true interior, personal mortification.

It is all too easy to reduce your speaking to a projection of yourself, instead of making it an instrument for communicating yourself. To avoid this we must "translate" what we feel, bearing in mind as far as possible the person whom we are addressing.

6 The *second sign* of maturity is the energy to do things according to what our conscience sees or perceives.

This measures the second possibility that one has of achieving dialogue as the mutual communication of existence.

In GS this second possibility takes the form of what are called "initiatives."

Initiatives have an extremely important meaning in the life-dialogue that is GS. The Christian proposal does not draw us out of existence, but engages us in it. It is addressed to the whole of our life, and the fact that it can be applied to every phenomenon of life reveals the clearest experience of its truth. In GS initiatives are conceived specifically as the application, in common, of the Christian proposal to one of the needs and experiences that make up the fabric of human life.

Therefore, in theory, there is no limit to possible initiatives in GS. Their growth points to the vitality of those who sustain them. Their abundance makes it easy for many to be helped in "doing," as they offer a wide choice and respond to different needs, characters, levels of awareness, generosity, opinions, and tastes.

There are moments of common prayer (the Mass, the divine office, hymns, retreats, etc.), cultural debates, charitable works, newspapers, theatre, cinema, trips, and sports: all these expressions of youthful vitality must find their place in the *raggio*. We can list two levels of commitment in this field:

a. Taking part in the initiatives

None of these is compulsory, but wholesale disinterest is certainly a half-hearted way to live the *raggio*.

We need to be trained in dialogue, and taking up an initiative broadens and stabilizes an openness to dialogue. It is good to start by choosing those initiatives we feel more capable of, so as to become more easily dedicated to them.

But it is just as necessary to have the courage to risk a commitment to more decidedly significant initiatives such as prayer and reflection in the first place; these, by their very nature, do not exclude commitment to other initiatives but rather lend them meaning.

b. Launching initiatives

Commitment stimulates inventiveness, and even people with lesser talents can be much more productive regarding new ideas and initiatives than more intelligent but more laid-back individuals.

New initiatives are always the barometer of existing vitality: we should not stifle or suppress this vitality out of fear of the necessary effort or risk involved.

7 *The third sign* of maturity is the capacity to take on responsibilities within the community.

This is the point where the person is wholly engaged in self-communication, and dialogue touches his or her deepest potential.

In *GS*, the more responsibilities are created the more we have a living dialogue, a commitment to sharing our lives. So we must pay attention to all possible aspects of each initiative, to all the varied problems, to all the organizational structures, so that everyone can find a job in his or her appropriate place.

Concreteness

1 Dialogue is life

Life is not ideas, feelings, and inventiveness, though these are expressions of it. Life springs up and is built on a well-determined terrain, on something concrete. What do we call that from which our person emerges at every moment? We call it our situation. We are students, who live in a "scholastic" situation: so the dialogue in the *raggio* must spring from a student or school situation. Even the way and the time that we eat and our leisure time depend on school life: in these years a youngster's life is rooted in the school situation.

The surroundings in which a high-school student's freedom is most solicited and decisively affected are created by the school situation.

So it is there above all that we need to reach that student with our proposal.

The *raggio* will be focused on that specific situation, it will be the *raggio* of that particular school. So the basic activity of *GS* is the school *raggio*.

Once we have settled on where the *raggio* originates and acts, we must still be sure to discover and respect the practical situation and concrete experiences that will make an educative activity realistic in those surroundings.[2]

2 Needs in the student milieu

a. Tireless proposal. The masses are distracted, far away from our concerns. We must never flag; we must reach out, form relationships, propose, solicit. Our supreme duty before God is to communicate our Christian reality to everyone. It will not be our fault if few turn up; it will be our fault if, through lack of initiative, we have not invited them. In the long run the *number* who respond will be a means of measuring our vitality. Normally there are too few of us because we do too little.

b. Flexibility. Life in the youth environment is extremely volatile (we do not develop detailed annual plans because after two weeks they turn out to be abstract schemes). If we must have some provisional scheme, let it be specific on some essential points, but always adaptable; any rigidity would be introversion and self-centredness.

c. Differentiation. Age, class spirit, groups of friends; all these often determine the typical situations in the broader school environment.

We must be aware of these situations, so that we can use them, too, as a starting point for our proposal.

Thus, for example, we need:

– to think of some activities for older students that differ from those for students starting high school;
– to introduce the initiative of the proposal into class activities if there is a lively spirit in that class;
– to remember that one cannot expect to get other people's attention unless we give them ours intelligently and wholeheartedly.

d. Deeply felt responsibility. Taking up a responsibility, even a minor one, as well as increasing our energy, helps us to take risks in defence of the common good and to care for the ideal as our own. Therefore it will be necessary to:

– appoint a leader in each group, assisted by a deputy (who can later take over the responsibilities of leader) and a secretary to see to technical organization (announcements, activities, etc.);
– appoint someone responsible for the life of GS for every floor or sector of the school and, most important, for each class;

– appoint someone responsible for each initiative (central ones, such as the student paper, tourism, and charitable work; and particular and one-off ones, such as a collection of funds or a conference) for the whole school, with, perhaps, an assistant in each class.

e. Sociability. To share in your own environment you must be involved in school life. Here we need to stress three aspects:

– when faced with anti-Catholic attitudes in some teachers or in required texts you must very quickly and constantly help your classmates to review the matter and clarify its meaning from the Catholic angle. This can be done through extemporized discussions after school or by organizing a debate with a group or with the whole class. To take on a teacher in class, you need maximum discretion and certitude, so best get advice first.

– when faced with attitudes and events that affect the climate of the class or a group you must affirm your own Christian position without presumption, without aggression, but with conviction and decisiveness.

– many schools have student associations and school magazines. We must be careful: an incautious and immature contribution is not a contribution; it leads to confusion. There is no need for thirty members of the *raggio* to attend the meetings of an association; only those who are able to make a real contribution should attend, otherwise we will be wasting our time and others'. Taking part means making a contribution: we must first be aware of being Christians to bear witness in an environment in which we inevitably compare ourselves with what we are not. We must participate without being naïve or childish, which would amount to being presumptuous.

3 Needs of the students as persons

Here we recall the great rule that expresses the spirit of complete openness proper to charity: to adapt ourselves to others. So above all:

– we must apply ourselves to inviting people. To apply ourselves means knowing how to use sensitivity, understanding, and trust, but above all to take note of the free possibility of enrichment for ourselves that is present in the person of another who listens. This awareness will make it easier for us to pay attention to the other as he or she is, in his or her unique personality.

- we must take special note of someone who comes for the first time, because this is one of our greatest responsibilities. We must follow them up, not abandon them after the first step; follow them up with extreme respect and fidelity.
- we must not take for granted that others are always aware of the meaning of what we do. We must constantly recall the motive for our meeting, the motive and the spirit of our dialogue. This will also help us to consciously keep our commitment ever fresh. To this end it is wise to hold a *raggio* every so often to clarify once more the meaning of our meeting ("stock-taking"). We must keep on repeating things, because that's what the difficult job of education requires.
- the *raggio* must be felt as something open to all: this means, on the one hand, that we must organize the *raggio* so as to open what comes up to all as much as possible, with criteria to be decided each time; on the other hand, "open to all" means not preventing anyone from being able to relate. Personal attention is only such if it is open to all and all are open to it.

And be careful not to become bogged down in merely personal preferences, because this would be reckless self-limitation.

4 Needs of the students as youth to be educated

In high school, students are still in need of education, and they are in the most characteristic moment of that process. This is one of the most misunderstood and rejected realities, yet it is the most crucial for their personal reality.

Two important, extremely practical guidelines should be followed:

a. Stress the value of concrete things, even though they seem to be minor details:
- prepare the room well before time, and leave it in order afterwards;
- be punctual;
- maintain order in the discussions: avoid wandering off the point, suppress the desire to say everything you have in mind;
- speak clearly in the meetings, so that it is easier for others to pay attention;
- pray together;
- have a sense of the others present while singing, etc.

b. Respond to a youngster's need for guidance:

Every *raggio* and, if possible, all the larger initiatives must have:

– a priest as chaplain, to animate and safeguard the Christian life of the members;

– a person in charge, a more mature person who has already had an intense experience of the spirit of *GS*, to animate and safeguard this spirit in the student participants.

Then each one, insofar as he or she has lived a genuine experience, can help in educating companions; the less one gives in to weak-minded presumption and sentimentalism the more one will be helpful.

THE DEVELOPMENT OF THE *GS* EXPERIENCE: A PATH FOR ITS DEVELOPMENT

In its every expression, *GS*, if it is to be truly such, must take up the dimensions of the Gospel, in particular, according to the basic law of "communion of oneself," which opens up the person to everyone and seeks to converge all things towards unity.

But it is in particular, practical facts that the human spirit senses vividly and learns those ideals that govern the structure and conduct of its existence. A serious concern of *GS* is to cultivate this *inductive activity*, if it intends to be a place of education.

So *GS* sets in motion some *concrete forms of activity, that it proposes as indispensable,* to educate youth to develop the fundamental dimensions of the Christian experience without any ambiguity.

While one is left completely free regarding all other initiatives, those listed below are essential for the reality of *GS*. Therefore, all *GS* students must try to take part in them.

The Conquest of Culture

1 Culture and Christ

Culture is the experience of a reality that explains all things. Christ is that reality for man.

For youth, to walk within the experience of Christ as the One who clarifies all things is the most acute and evocative aspect of one's growth into a full personality, a convinced and responsible personality.

The most fascinating and intense task of *GS* is to help this growth.

2 An effective method

a. A youth must experience the Christian criterion as the one that clarifies all that attracts, engages or affects his or her intelligence. This is the concept of *reviewing* the cultural complex. This complex can be divided, in broad terms, into two areas:

– Facts. Youths encounter facts that demand a meaningful and global interpretation;

– Ideas. Ideas or, in other words, judgments on the facts, reach youth as ready-made interpretations, preconceived human reflections. These interpretative judgments, too, are offered to the youngster's conscience for judgment.

b. The source of these two categories of encounters to which the intelligence is called to give a global meaning can, for a student, be described thus:

– *school*, through what he or she studies. Here the problem is particularly serious in a scholastic situation like the Italian one, which is constitutionally incapable of giving a global meaning to the subjects that youth study. For the most part they end up insensitive to ideal values;

– the world of the *here and now*, the life that pulsates around us daily.

In these two supremely important sectors that attract and inevitably influence young people's consciences *GS* must show, in action, the ever-present measure of the Christian criterion of evaluation (measure, from the Latin "metior," which lies at the root of "mens," the mind).

The reviews of studies and of current affairs (the here and now) are the two poles within which *GS* imparts a cultural education to young people.

3 Initiatives

In *GS* a "committee" of people work as a team to oversee the cultural initiatives of the whole movement. This does not mean that there cannot be individual initiatives; there must be.

a. Study review

I We prepare notes to help students tackle, from a Christian viewpoint, the problems and personalities they encounter in their normal course of studies. We call them *review sheets*. Every *raggio* should make use of this material, with the help of the person in charge of cultural matters, in the course of daily study and in the organization of meetings on the topic, etc.

II Students are invited to make a habit of studying together (supervised by someone in charge, at least at first). Some of those in charge of cultural matters (graduates or senior undergraduates) should carry out a thorough and timely review of the material studied, visiting these groups and showing them, while they go over the day's lessons, how Christianity brings out great meaning in all topics. This work becomes all the more urgent when – as more and more frequently happens – the school "positively" contradicts the authentic Christian vision of reality. In this way truly systematic work is possible, since the review is done concurrently with the studies as they are presented in the curriculum and no precious time is wasted.

III If the need arises for clarifications and answers in broad areas of the school environment, lectures or lessons can be organized to explain the Christian position on specific problems generated by the subjects being studied. Programs systematically planned in advance, at the beginning of the year, do not attract anyone.

IV Textbooks whose fundamental approach is Catholic (unlike those normally found these days) are passed around among the students. Students, if they are helped, can then cross-check the assertions they hear at school or read in other textbooks.

V During summer vacations "study groups" in regular contact can probe some of the more critical problems that emerged in the course of the year; each group can then offer the results of its research for use by all, using suitable means.

b. Review of current events

I When events or expressions of an outlook that can particularly mark students arise, *GS* takes a *specific stand*, by communicating, where appropriate, a clear value judgment to the whole student environment, through the printed word, debates, meetings, etc.

II In *GS* a group with a particular interest in this aspect of the Christian problem collects all the relevant documentation (books, articles, films, data, etc.). Any *GS* student can report his or her discoveries in this field. From time to time the group in charge will, in its turn, report on any new documentation to the *raggio* groups; normally this material will provide an idea for the *raggio* meetings.

III Another way of taking a stand on particular problems that current events suggest to students is the organization of interviews with outstanding Christian personalities who are experts in such events or problems.

IV Examples of human experiences interpreted or solved in the light of Christian values are proposed systematically to the youngsters:
- a *book of the month*, chosen carefully from among the more significant on a topic;
- *dossiers on converts*, which give in summary form the witnesses of great people who have converted to Christianity. A bibliography is included so that those who wish can study the matter more deeply;
- *during Advent*: Christian experiences of great personalities well-known to students, which document the human expectation of Christ in our world;
- *the Library* collects only works selected for these aims.

V Every year *GS*, in collaboration with other Catholic Youth movements, launches a big student convention on a theme of general interest, regarding which the Catholic point of view will be proposed to all schoolmates.

Charitable Activity

1 The spirit of charitable activity

Life should be a total sharing, but distraction, fear, convenience, the impediments of the environment, and malevolence empty life of the value of charity.

To train ourselves to fill this void continually, to create an outlook of charity, the most humble and effective method is to start to give some part of our free time expressly and willingly as a sharing in other people's lives.

It is essential to commit ourselves through a physical sacrifice in order to influence our outlook.

The charitable activity of *GS* is understood as a contribution to sharing in social or personal situations of hardship, not to reforming them.
- in other words, it is to fulfill (as other duties, parents, and the extent of our goodwill permit) at least a small part of our supreme duty, which is that of placing ourselves in community

and sharing life, up to death, just as Jesus Christ did and as the Church does.

2 So to share life is not to endure a presence passively, but to accept it. This implies an ongoing initiative on our part, expressed in a capacity to be open before the wealth of life represented by the person of another.

3 What is to be committed in charitable activity?

Something of yourself.

From the maximum: someone who gives all his or her free time, or almost all, and all that he or she can physically offer; to the minimum: someone who can – or wants to – give only money, the fruit of a sacrifice, to support the activity of others.

4 Practical fields of activity

There are many fields, depending on creativity, sensitivity, and circumstances, provided that our motive remain clear, a pure sharing with people.

So, in addition to the initiative already going on in the "Bassa"[3] suburbs of Milan, any traditional form of charitable activity can be re-evaluated.

Missionary Action

1 The aim of missionary action

To create sensitivity in the students for the deepest aspect of charity: in other words, the supreme duty we have of sharing the most universal need, that of discovering and following Christ and the Church.

To create a sense of worldwide responsibility: this is the goal we must attain. The ideal would be to arouse in students' minds the need for a new perspective in studying, choosing a profession, in conceiving the road of life: a perspective that goes beyond the limits of personal convenience or taste, or one's own career, and extends to the awareness of being useful to the world and history.

2 Ways to follow

a. Accomplish specific gestures, whose meaning will very soon educate us not to sense anything of ours as *belonging to us*, but as destined for the whole world.

b. Establish an ever more vital contact with one part of this world, so that interior concern may, in an increasingly positive way, take on concrete form.

c. Get to know the essential aspects of the missionary problem.

d. Make contact with people already dedicated to the problem: missionaries or specialists; above all, those born in non-Christian civilizations.

This is not a matter of numbers and data. It is above all a question of getting to know other civilizations; in other words, other great conceptions and experiences of life, so as to compare them with respect and vigilance to the Church experience, and thus to discover the possibilities of dialogue and to seek, with utmost responsibility, ways to favour the beginning of such a dialogue.

3 Practical means

– Insist at all times that the youngsters not receive any money without deducting part of it, little or much depending on individual generosity, as concrete witness of a concern for the whole world and its happiness, which means the spread of the Kingdom of God. (This is the ancient, spontaneous concept of tithes, basic for a true Christian awareness).

– GS already has a deep bond with a faraway country: Brazil. This bond consists in:

a. the organized visits of persons (university students in charge of GS) who help meet the needs of the Christian community there for a fixed term;

b. the hospitality that the GS community offers students from Brazil, which aims at deepening an understanding;

c. the publication of an international magazine, Okara, which aims at creating a dialogue between our community and youth in Brazil (but we foresee spreading this magazine to other countries, too);

d. the high point of the initiative, which lies in those of us who have decided to dedicate themselves, without any time limit, to the service of the Church in the missionary world. These persons are sensed in GS as the "front line" of the whole community that they express. Their educative function for GS is irreplaceable.

– at all levels the initiative favours vigorous and shared attention to the missionary dimension in the raggios and offers the opportunities to converse with those who have already had an experience of this kind (those returning from Brazil or those about to go there).

– we spread the practice of reading books that clearly propose the idea of mission: the reading of missionary magazines; the

helping of missionary initiatives and associations (such as the Student Missionary League and World Mission Sunday).
– in the *raggio* we favour encounters with missionaries and students from mission countries.

Tangible Unity: The GS Centre

1 Meaning
This is the most decisive factor in the whole education of *GS*, as the guide on a youngster's road to maturity.

2 Origin
The priests that the bishop appoints for *GS* form the hub of the Centre as a guide to Christian experience.

Around them are collaborators, lay people who are solidly grounded in the *GS* spirit.

3 Convergence
The Centre is where the deepest unity of all the *raggios* and all the initiatives is understood and expressed.

Refusing this convergence without an exceptionally serious motive would amount to blocking, and therefore crippling, the Christian testimony.

4 Participation
Both at the level of the *raggio* and at the general level, all the associations should have their followers participate in a steadfast witness in the environment, a *unitary* witness, at least as far as this is possible.

The *GS* centre does not try to impose itself on other realities; it is rather the concrete manifestation of ecclesial charity.

Every association remains wholly itself: before the world of the environment, however, nothing exists but Christian unity.

THE GOAL: A NEW ENVIRONMENT

Of all that we have described up to now, the real and living result is the creation of a *new environment* within the student milieu.

1 The *Christian ideal*, sensed as the only answer to life experience as a whole, dominates this environment.

Free adherence, at all times, is the only condition for participation: there is no enrolment and there are no statutory obligations. It is a movement, not an association.

This freedom is generated by accepting the Christian presence of others, by participating in the *Christian community*.

This community has a fundamental, nurturing focal point: the *raggio* meeting. But the locus of its life is broader: first the world of one's school, then the wider student world.

It is the beginning in time and space of that *new civilization* to which Christianity inevitably calls man. Through this real beginning one is educated in an approach that the whole of life and the broader world that frames it are destined to participate in.

2 Some fundamental responsibilities must be clearly set out for the life of the community to function properly.

In each group there is:
- a *raggio* leader and a *deputy*, who represent the unity and continuity of the community life
- a secretary to take charge of the organizational matters
In each group activity:
- a person in charge of organization
- collaborators, explicitly appointed and adequate in number for the scope of the initiative.

3 All groups and all their activities have the *GS* Centre as their point of reference, animator, unifier, and coordinator.

The fundamental structures of the life of the Centre are:
- *The Presiding Group* (Central Chaplains, President, Vice-president, General Secretary and central secretaries, General Director of the Initiatives, and the General Director of the *raggio*). The Presiding Group has ultimate responsibility for everything;
- The *Central Commissions* of the *GS* initiatives (culture, charitable work, missions), who are responsible for directing initiatives in the movement;
- The *GS Diocesan Council* (Chaplains, Presidents of each town, with the corresponding Central Directors).

NOTES

CHAPTER ONE

1 Matthew 10:32. Most of the biblical passages are from the English version of *The Jerusalem Bible* (Garden City: Doubleday, 1966).

The other passages have been paraphrased and maintained in quotation marks, as Luigi Giussani did in the original.

2 Ephesians 1:4, 6.

3 1 John 4:19.

4 John 6:44; Matthew 9:38.

5 John 14:6.

6 Jeremiah 31:3.

7 Matthew 28:20.

8 Luke 10:25, 27.

9 Luke 9:24.

10 Act 4, scene 5, translation by Louise Morgan Sill. New Haven: Yale University Press 1916.

11 Genesis 12:1; *See also* Genesis 12:3.

12 Genesis 1:28.

13 *See* John 8:24, 34.

14 *See* Matthew 18:19–20.

15 Luke 23:34.

16 Act 4, scene 5.

17 John 10:30.

18 John 17:23.

CHAPTER TWO

1 Baruch 3:38.

2 The school is the students' main ambit. The experience of the school *raggio*, then, tends to extend the life of the *raggio* into the holiday period and into areas where the youngsters spend these holidays: this is the "summer *raggio*," which arises in the main resort areas, where *GS* students meet and mix with other vacationing friends on the beach or in hotels. [Translator's note: this note was in the original Italian edition].

3 Low-income suburban neighbourhoods in the southern reaches of Milan where *GS* students carried out their charitable work in the late 50s and early 60s.

Traces of the Christian Experience

To the grown-ups who know how to speak,
To the young who know how to listen.

Gioventù Studentesca, 1960

1 Formulation of the Human Problem

Even after sharing their lives with Jesus for such a long time, after the disaster of Calvary and the mystery of Easter, after all that, the apostles understood little of Him. Only a few hours before His ascent into Heaven, they still asked Him when he would establish the Kingdom of Israel, such as everyone conceived it at that time: a kingdom of earthly and political power.

"So when they had come together they asked Him, 'Lord will you at this time restore the Kingdom of Israel?'"[1]

If they did not understand Him, why did they follow Him? And among them were those who had left wife, children, home, boat and nets, offices, business. Why did they follow Him?

They followed Christ because He had become the focus of their affections. Why?

Where they had been unaware and confused, they were enlightened, for Christ was the only one in whose words they felt their whole human experience understood and their needs taken seriously, clarified. Thus, for instance, those very people who used to believe that their only need was bread began to understand that "Man does not live by bread alone."

Christ introduces Himself to them in just this way, as *an Other*, who surprisingly moves in their direction, helps them, explains their troubles to them; He cures them if they are crippled or blind, heals their souls, responds to their needs, is within their experience. But what are their experiences? Their experiences, their needs, are their very selves, those men and women, their own human nature.

Thus Christ is right here, in my attitude and disposition as a human being, in my way, that is, as one who expects, awaits something, because I sense that I am entirely wanting. He has joined me. He has proposed Himself to my original needs.

Hence, to meet Christ we must first formulate our human problem seriously.

First, we must open ourselves to ourselves. In other words, we must be acutely aware of our experiences and look on the humanity within us with sympathy; we must take into consideration who we really are. To take into consideration means to take seriously what we experience, *everything* we experience, to discover every aspect, to seek the complete meaning.

We must be very careful, because all too easily we do not start from our true experience; that is, from our experience in its entirety and authenticity. We often identify our experience with partial impressions, truncating it, as often happens with affective matters, when we fall in love or dream about the future.

Even more often we confuse our experience with the prejudices or schemes that we absorb from our environment, perhaps unawares. Therefore, instead of opening up to that attitude of expectation, sincere attention, and dependence that our experience suggests and fervently demands, we impose categories and explanations that constrict and distress our experience, while presuming to resolve it.

The myth that "scientific progress one day will solve all our needs" is the modern formula of this presumption, a wild and repugnant presumption, because it does not consider or even know our real needs. It refuses to observe our experience clearly and to accept what it means to be human, with all the needs that this implies. For this reason modern civilization causes us to move blindly between this desperate presumption and darkest despair.

SOLITUDE

A vital cue comes to us from the situation of the apostles as narrated to us in verses 9 to 11 in the first chapter of the Acts.

Christ has left and they remain there still and astonished. Hope has vanished and solitude falls upon them just as darkness and cold descend on the earth after sunset. The more we discover our needs, the more we become aware that we cannot resolve them on our own. Nor can others, people like us. A sense of *powerlessness* accompanies every serious experience in our lives.

This sense of powerlessness generates solitude. True solitude does not come from being physically alone but from the discovery that a fundamental problem of ours cannot find its solution in us or in others.

We can well say that the sense of solitude is borne in the very heart of every serious commitment to our own humanity. Those who believe they have found the solution to a great need of theirs in something or someone, only to have this something or someone disappear or prove incapable of resolving this need, can understand this. We are alone in our needs, in our need to be and to live intensely, like one alone in the desert. All he or she can do is wait until someone appears. And human persons will certainly not provide the solution because it is precisely their needs that must be resolved.

COMMUNITY

The apostles returned to the place where Christ had ascended into heaven and they stayed together (Acts 1:12–14).

One who truly discovers and lives the experience of powerlessness and solitude does not remain alone. Only one who has experienced powerlessness to its depths, and hence personal solitude, feels close to others and is easily drawn to them. Like someone lost, without shelter in a storm, he or she feels his or her cry at one with the cries of others, his or her anxiety and expectation at one with the anxieties and expectations of all others.

Only one who truly experiences helplessness and solitude stays with other people without self-interest, calculation, or imposition, yet at the same time without "following the crowd" passively, submitting, or becoming a slave of society.

You can claim to be seriously committed to your own human experience only when you sense this community with others, with anyone and everyone, without frontiers and discrimination, for we live our commitment to what is most deeply within us and therefore common to all. You are truly committed to your own human experience when, saying "I", you live this "I" so simply and profoundly that you feel fraternally bonded to any other person's "I." God's answer will reach only the person committed in such a way.

It must immediately be pointed out that this solidarity with all of humanity is achieved in a particular place. Even in the Acts (see I:13, 23–6) the community of the apostles is born in a very specific situation. They did not choose the place or the people. They found themselves there almost by chance and their whole life depended on this fact.

This is how our personal humanity is born, shaped, and nourished, in a particular *setting*: we find ourselves in it; we don't choose it.

Our effort to understand the entire setting and offer our sense of community to all the people in that setting, measures the openness of our human commitment and is commensurate with the sincerity of our commitment to all humanity. It is not up to us to exclude anyone from the experience of our human life; only God can make that choice and He does so through the situation in which He places us. Otherwise it would be a private matter on our part, a selfish looking-inward; we would be taking advantage of a given situation through our own preconceived schemes.

AUTHORITY

Peter, the most representative person in the community, stands up and speaks, and he is heeded (see Acts I:15–22).

In our particular milieu some individuals have a greater sensitivity to the human experience; *in fact* they develop a deeper understanding of any given situation and of others; *in fact* they are more likely to influence the movement that builds a community. They live our experience more intensely and with a greater commitment. We all feel that they are more representative of us. With them we feel closer to, and stay more willingly in community with, others. To acknowledge this phenomenon is to be loyal to our own humanity, a duty spurred by wisdom.

When we discover ourselves helpless and alone, our humanity spurs us to come together. If we meet someone who better feels and understands our experience, suffering, needs, and expectations, we naturally are led to follow that person and become his or her disciple. In that sense, such persons naturally constitute *authority* for us even if they do not carry special rights or titles. Naturally, above all, it is one who most loyally lives or understands the human experience who becomes an authority.

Thus authority is born as a wealth of experience that imposes itself on others. It generates freshness, wonder, and respect. Inevitably, it is attractive; it is evocative. Not to value the presence of this *effective authority* that His Being places in every setting is to cling pettily to our own limits. The Jews said of Christ: "This is one who has authority" and they abandoned the schemes of the Pharisees to follow Him.

The encounter with this natural authority develops our sensitivity and our conscience; it helps us to discover better our nature and what we aspire to from the depths of our present poverty.

PRAYER

Verse 14 of Acts I shows us the community of the apostles awaiting what Christ had promised. "All these joined together in assiduous prayer."

Those who discover their own helplessness live in community and are aware that their lives are shared with others only when they have *the presentiment of something beyond their own situations* that can resolve these situations. A community can come about only when there is a common expectancy (even a man and woman who truly love each other have this unshakeable presentiment; otherwise they do not take their relationship seriously).

Our experiences, when really taken seriously, are painful, for they make us discover that we are full of needs, unresolved problems, sorrow, and ignorance. If these experiences are truly taken seriously, they unequivocally require something "else," something "beyond"; that is, they possess a genuine religious dimension.

If our experiences are taken seriously they are an authentic prophecy (expectancy, hope) of what we do not yet have.

What we still lack is the *meaning* of all our experiences. And we await it, perhaps unconsciously.

If we are truly aware of this expectancy, of our human incapacity and of what our nature relentlessly tells us, then this expectancy is bound to become *prayer*. It will become prayer to a mysterious Other who will be able to help and will provide a solution. It will become prayer to that God who elicits our question and who will provide the answer.

Thus, prayer is simple petition, entreaty; our most simple, heartfelt, and fundamental act of human awareness. The most realistic person is the one who prays: that person takes his or her experience seriously.

Prayer is also *a plea made together, in common.* The discovery of our powerlessness to achieve happiness is also the discovery of what we have most in common with all others: this powerlessness is what is most human in each of us.

Thus, even the disposition to await the help of that Other, is shared by all; it is communital by its very nature, so much so that no one can have that disposition without feeling himself or herself as "one heart" with everyone.

2 The Encounter with Christ

What we have described as human experience is the prerogative of all men and women.

The only genius who grasped all the different human factors, brought them to light, and revealed their definitive meaning by giving them value in an unimaginable and unexpected way was Jesus Christ. The historical encounter with this man constitutes an encounter with the resolving and clarifying point of view of human experience.

It is precisely this encounter that we wish to attain once again. Hence let us examine the initial moments in which it emerged. Here is the first historical record of the fact: "On the following day as John stood again with two of his disciples, Jesus passed, and John stared hard at Him and said, "Look, there is the lamb of God." Hearing this, the two disciples followed Jesus. Jesus turned around, saw them following and said, "What do you want?" They answered, "Rabbi (which means Teacher), where do you live?" "Come and see," He replied; and so they went and saw where He lived, and stayed with Him the rest of the day. It was about the tenth hour."[1]

One of the two is the historian narrating the fact and, now, as a centenarian, he remembers the moment in detail, for it marked the beginning of a new life for him.

The story proceeds with the encounters of Philip and Nathanael. The latter was the "old fellow" in the company, a shrewd individual, always on his guard not to be cheated by anyone. "Come and see," they say to him. This is always the most persuasive argument. Jesus sees Nathanael arriving and He says to him: "Here comes a true Israelite incapable of deceit." "How do you know me?" replies Nathanael, almost as if he does not want to be flattered. "Before Philip called you I saw you under the fig-tree." And Nathanael yields immediately: "Rabbi, you are the Son of God."[2]

At this moment this man's reputation began to emerge among the people. After their initial astonishment, the disciples are so struck by what He says and the way He looks at them, that they accept Him immediately; that is, they place their trust in Him. The following chapter of the Gospel tells about the miracle at the wedding of Cana and ends with these words: "Jesus performed the first miracle. And his disciples believed in him."[3] This shows that the event developed over time.

If those disciples had not seen Him again they would have forgotten that strange encounter, even though they had acknowledged Him as the Messiah since the first meeting. Instead, to re-encounter Him was like deepening an original impression. They reinforced their belief in this continuous convergence of impressions and feelings. Not that previously they had been insincere or non-believing; rather, they followed the guiding principle of human awareness that implies this development.

Thus, even at other times, after the wedding of Cana, the Gospel notes: "and His disciples believed in Him." A depth is achieved that brings one to that degree of confidence and conviction where one is finally persuaded: *one is certain*.

Let us now single out those *aspects of Christ's personality* that were and are exceptional to their eyes and ours.

AN EXTRAORDINARY PRESENCE

Above all Christ shows authoritativeness and superiority on every occasion.

Let us try to imagine those people who for weeks had seen Him return to the seashore, and then for three successive years continuously witnessed extraordinary episodes ... until some abandoned everything to follow Him always and everywhere.

They were used to troublemakers, especially in those years when everyone awaited the Messiah, and surely troublemakers arouse alarm. But Jesus lies outside the usual scheme of things. He does not incite the people to take up arms against the Roman Empire. The leaders will be most preoccupied with stalking Him to catch Him out and trip him up, thus unwittingly bearing witness.

It is midday, and Christ retires to a small house to eat, but the people crowd the entrance. He continues to speak. The Pharisees are in the first row. They bring Jesus a man who has been paralysed for twenty years. Not being able to get him through the doorway, they let him in through the roof just behind Jesus. Jesus turns and says: "Be confident, son, your sins are forgiven." Immediately the Pharisees think: "This man is blasphemous; who can forgive sins except God?" Turning from the poor ill man to the people Jesus says: "Now which of these is easier to say, 'Your sins are forgiven' or 'Get up and walk?' But to prove to you that the Son of Man has authority on earth to forgive sins, I say to you: 'Get up, pick up your bed and go home.'" And the man gets up and makes his way amid the understandably loud cries of the crowd.[4] And such events occur daily: "He arrived in the evening tired of healing" is a refrain in the Gospel.[5]

THE RULER OF NATURE

Those who follow Him witness His exceptional command over nature.

"Then He got into a boat, followed by His disciples. Without warning a storm broke over the lake, so violent that the waves were breaking right over the boat. But He was asleep. So they went to Him and woke Him saying: 'Save us, Lord, we are going down!' And He said to them: 'Why are you so frightened, you men of little faith?' And with that, He stood up and rebuked the winds and the sea; and all was calm again. The men were astounded and said: 'Whatever kind of man is this? Even the winds and the sea obey him.'"[6]

HE KNOWS AND UNDERSTANDS US

But the most persuasive power, which made Nathanael yield and which takes hold of each of us is this mastery over our minds and hearts: His understanding. It is normal for Him to read one's past, to discern one's intentions so that everyone feels that even the secret parts of their human personalities belong to Him.

He feels tired and sits near a well and a woman comes to draw water. "Give me some water," Jesus asks her, and she begins to tease Him in a rough, tactless manner. "If you knew who is asking you: 'Give me some water,' you would ask Him for some. The well is deep and you haven't got a bucket, how can you give me water? … Go and call your husband. " "But I have no husband." "You are right to say 'I have no husband'; for although you have had five, the one you have now is not your husband."⁷ And she relents.

When people met prostitutes or tax collectors they had to keep their distance so as not to be contaminated by them; this was a rather clever way to make moral law penetrate thick heads. But He behaved in a completely different way. He even ate with these people.

He entered Jericho and was making his way through the town when a man, whose name was Zacchaeus, one of the senior tax collectors and a wealthy man, made his appearance. He was eager to see the kind of man Jesus was, but being so short, he could not see Jesus for the crowd. So he ran on ahead and climbed a sycamore tree to catch a glimpse of Jesus, who was to pass that way. When Jesus reached the spot He looked up and spoke: "Zacchaeus, come down. Hurry, because I must stay at your house today." And Zacchaeus hurried down and welcomed Him joyfully. Everyone complained when they saw what was happening. "He has gone to stay at a sinner's house," they said. But Zacchaeus stood his ground and said to the Lord, "Look, sir, I am going to give half my property to the poor, and if I have cheated anybody I will pay him back four times the amount."⁸

Before Him there is no barrier. He easily penetrates the complicated tangle of the human heart, by surprise or intuition. It is as if what I own is also His. Nothing disarms us or makes us yield with a sense of total abandonment as much as being discovered and understood.

LORD OF THE WORD

He had an irresistible, intelligent way of discussing matters. The Pharisees and the Scribes were renowned for their dialectic; however, before Him they were powerless.

Then the Pharisees went away to devise a way to trap Him in what He said. And they sent their disciples to Him, together with the Herodians, to say, "Master, we know that you are an honest man and teach the way of God in an honest way, and that you are not afraid of anyone, because a man's rank means nothing to you. Tell us your opinion, then. Is it permissible to pay taxes to Caesar or not?" But Jesus was aware of their malice and replied, "You hypocrites! Why do you set this trap for me? Let me see the money you pay the tax with." They handed him a denarius, and he said, "Whose head is this? Whose name?" "Caesar's," they replied. He then said to them, "Very well, give back to Caesar what belongs to Caesar – and to God what belongs to God." This reply took them by surprise, and they left Him alone and went away.

At daybreak He appeared in the temple again; and as all the people came to Him, He sat down and began to teach them.

The Scribes and Pharisees brought a woman who had been caught committing adultery; and making her stand there in full view of everybody, they said to Jesus, "Master, this woman was caught in the very act of committing adultery, and Moses has ordered us in the Law to condemn women like this to death by stoning. What have you to say?" They asked Him this as a test, looking for something to use against Him. But Jesus bent down and started writing on the ground with His finger. As they persisted with their question, He looked up and said, "If there is one of you who has not sinned, let him be the first to throw a stone at her." Then He bent down and wrote on the ground again. When they heard this they went away one by one, beginning with the eldest.[10]

The trap is sprung and it challenges their hypocrisy.

The Master's word is so compelling and so difficult not to take seriously that it is overwhelming and even paralysing: "The police went back to the chief priests and Pharisees who said to them, 'Why haven't you brought Him?' The police replied, 'No one has ever spoken like Him.'"[11]

THE GOOD SHEPHERD

But another characteristic distinguishes Him. Those powerful people who can fathom our psyche, who speak from their chairs of learning, are seldom very good. He, instead, "took a little child and set him by his side."[12] And again, "Now soon afterward He went to a town called Nain, accompanied by His disciples and a great number of people. When He was near the gate of the town it happened that a dead man was being carried out for burial, the only son of his mother, and she was a widow. And a considerable number of the townspeople were with her. When the Lord saw her He felt sorry for her. 'Do not cry,' He said. Then He went up and put His hand on the bier and the bearers stood still, and He said, 'Young man, I tell you to get up,' and the dead man sat up and began to talk, and Jesus gave him to his mother."[13]

The experience of goodness is the encounter with an attitude that values and enhances us and gives us hope for what we shall become; it is "peace on earth," for God is good. And God is good because He saves us. Redemption is the announcement of the positive in life.

Before those who see Him there so tall and powerful, He inclines himself over a flower in the field and describes its "garb"; He always speaks kindly and sensitively of the sun and rain. Not: "How dreary, it's raining today," or "the sun is really bothering me." And His attention towards man is full of infinite understanding, unreservedly friendly and affectionate: even all the hairs of your head are counted.

He has compassion for those in grief and is unable to dine without first having healed. He cries over Lazarus and weeps over the city.

And He was human not only because of His fondness for nature or even the most insignificant details of an individual, or because He was so affectionate but also because He could share in human joy. It is particularly meaningful that He should attribute a special value to sharing a meal. The greatest act of His religion is identified with a meal. The kingdom is often compared to a banquet and the final glory is described as sitting at table with Abraham, Isaac, and Jacob.[14]

WHO IS THIS MAN?

It was only natural that the people who followed Him, particularly those who were with such an outstanding personality all the time, should have asked themselves: "Who is this man?"

Nicodemus, a learned and cultured man who lived the human experience intensely, immediately recognized that that man could only come from God.

But even the uncouth and illiterate people who left everything to follow Him did not behave differently. Romano Guardini observes: "They approach Him, listen to Him, come back and ultimately are impressed by a personality without compare. This impression gradually becomes a conviction: Jesus is superior to any other being."[15]

There is something inexplicable about Him, something we cannot quite grasp.

By sharing their lives with Christ it became obvious that it was only too natural, too right to trust Him. To oppose this evidence would be tantamount to going against oneself. Thus they were unable not to believe in Him simply because He may have made a statement that they did not understand: "in order to be coherent with what we have seen, to be coherent with ourselves, we have to accept even that which you say and yet we cannot understand. Only in you do we find our meaning." We could use these words to translate Peter's reasonable attitude in the episode described in chapter 6 of Saint John's Gospel.[16]

What is the difference between the excited crowd a few days before this episode and this small group of faithful followers, who are also enthusiastic but in a different way? The crowd sought Him for their own reasons and that is why, when He began to explain why He had come – an explanation that went beyond anyone's expectations – they left Him. They were more attached to their own limits than to the truth.

But the group of the faithful did not leave even though they did not understand. When they asked Him "Who are you?" and He answered mysteriously: "My Father and I are one," they accepted these words, even though they did not understand them.[17]

They would understand only on the day of the Pentecost, when they would be given a supernatural intelligence. As we have already observed, a few hours before He ascended into Heaven, they asked Him: "Master, when will you establish this Kingdom of Israel?"[18]

They understood very little even after His death and resurrection. But they preserved the mysterious answer because "He had spoken it."

THE ENCOUNTER TODAY

The very human disposition of the early faithful is still the same inevitable starting point today.

Christ is walking with the apostles and He happens upon a rock on the road: "Who do people say I am? ... And you, who do you say I am?" ... "You are Christ, Son of the living God." Peter pronounced words without understanding their true deep meaning. "You are fortunate because God and not your spirit suggested this to you. You are Peter and on this rock I shall build my Church."[19]

Even today Christianity is built on such a response. "Who do people say I am? Books, professors, film directors, freelance writers, party leaders, your father, your mother, your friends, who do they say I am? ... The first socialist, the first communist, the first liberal, the greatest religious genius, a visionary, a sorcerer, a lucky upstart."

"And you, who do you say I am?"

"And you, who do you say I am?" Our adult faith begins as a personal response to this question.

As long as the world exists, a human voice will confront the consciences of others and repeat the question, which is a proposal: "And you, who do you say I am?" And the answer: "You are God!" will spring in all times from the same disposition, from the same reasons, as did Peter's response.

It is extremely important to show how this fundamental dialogue, this decisive interlocutory choice, has a double component. First, there is the fact of an encounter – the encounter with the reality of Christ – an inevitable occasion, an indelible event in the life of the person who has this experience. Second, there is the attention paid to that fact, our "remaining" in that encounter, our commitment to it. This is not inevitable. This is our free choice.

COMMITMENT

But what does a commitment to an encounter regarding our existence mean, if we do not invest in it the powers of our sensitivity and awareness, that is, our very humanity.

Thus the discovery of Christ as a definitive reality to whom we must cling is a consequence of *sharing our lives* (*convivenza*). So the more we are aware of our own humanity, take seriously our experience, and live our existence intensely, the more our sharing our life with the historical reality of Christ will reveal the value of the encounter.

Christ proposes Himself with a question, but our response coincides with acknowledging Him as the only possible answer to our human pathway. A commitment to this path is still a condition for perceiving and understanding the gift of the encounter with Christ. The simpler the person, the more he or she lives that commitment, perhaps even unawares: thus it was with the apostles and the first disciples.

For us, reality is clouded and our eyes search for the light that gives it meaning. The voice of one Man in history reaches us: "I am that light ... He who follows me will not walk in darkness."[20] From the ocean of history a Word suddenly emerges that permeates all things and gives them form and coherence: "Dawn breaks and the morning star rises in your hearts."[21] But only by listening and by opening oneself to the world and to that light, by becoming sensitive to the former and receptive to the latter, can one understand that that Light is true.

The great adventure of human life is to reiterate that Man's proposal and to verify it. This is the great adventure that makes life and history pregnant with meaning, rather than a series of events. This is the great adventure that frees us from the feeling of futility and builds on the power of hope.

A passage from the Gospels captures the drama of this dialogue between human awareness and the presence of Christ magnificently:

"When they drew near to the village to which they were going, He made as if to go on; but they pressed Him to stay with them. 'It is nearly evening,' they said, 'and the day is almost over.' So He went to stay with them. Now while He was with them at table, he took the bread and said the blessing, then He broke it and handed it to them. And their eyes were opened and they recognized Him; but He had vanished from their sight. Then they said to each other, 'Did not our hearts burn within us as He talked to us on the road and explained the scriptures to us?'"[22]

Sharing that gesture, that is, the breaking of bread, became for them an enlightening idea that explained their journey with that unexpected foot traveller. By the light of that gesture they "verified" the entire experience of that encounter.

We can only ask ourselves one question now: why did that idea not dawn on them earlier? That the idea should emerge is a *gift*. It is *Grace*.

3 The Gift of the Spirit

THE EXPERIENCE OF THE DIVINE

"You cannot understand now. When the Spirit of Truth comes He will lead you to the complete truth."[1] The apostles had happened upon an exceptional, fascinating, and profoundly persuasive reality and accepted it, but they were not completely aware of what it was. They retained the words and respected them, but they measured them according to their own conception of things, without envisioning their hidden content. They reiterated definitions He gave of Himself without exactly understanding the mystery.

Saint Paul made a lucid analogy. An animal is aware of the presence of man and reacts to his behaviour and actions. And yet it does not grasp the reality that those actions convey. It remains at the margins of the reality that man represents: it "does not understand." An animal lacks the means to fathom the depths of thought and love and the tools to understand the message of another world because it lacks a human spirit. That is why it is a stranger even as it curls up at a man's feet or rubs against his legs or licks his hand: it does not share in human nature. And in the same way, concludes Saint Paul, "the depths of God can only be known by the Spirit of God."[2] Only one who possesses the Spirit has truly encountered Christ. As Saint Paul writes, "unless you possessed the Spirit of God you would not belong to Him,"[3] that is, you would be a stranger to Him, incapable of capturing His intimate makeup, His secret nature, of becoming familiar with His mystery.

Without the event of His Spirit, Christ can come across as a great man, an exceptional figure, unclassifiable by any standard; perhaps a strange figure who can persuade simple people irresistibly of their expectations, stimulate those with a passion for justice, threaten the structures that perpetuate the status quo: Christ was all these to His contemporaries. Or else He may appear so great as to become a moving or dramatic mythical figure, and this is perhaps the perception that characterizes our world's skeptical despair. Without the event of His Spirit, however, a person – whether an apostle or ourselves – remains in the dark, on the threshold of these perspectives. Without the event of the Spirit, Christ remains an enigmatic mysterious face for the human person; simply another voice that stands out in the chorus of voices, to remind us of our painful human expectancy. However, the interpretative key is still harboured within the ambiguous limits of the heart and the melancholic boundaries of human thought.

Thus Christ would be a new object to confront, a fresh risk to run blindly, and *not* a new criterion, *another* light, finally, a *new* answer. All life that is conscious, aware, cries out to us that our life's meaning here on earth is beyond our horizons. And so the encounter with Christ would be confined to the narrow bounds of the purely human experience and vision of reality – our culture – and condemned to oblivion, lost in the enigma of being and destiny, unfreed from its powerless, "unredeemed" state.

One day, however, "they heard what sounded like a powerful wind from heaven, the noise of which filled the entire house in which they were sitting ... and they were all filled with the Holy Spirit."[4] And so suddenly they understood who the man that they had followed was. The experience of their encounter with Him and the long, fervent, anxious, and uncertain period that they had shared with Him suddenly became another absolutely unforeseen and disconcerting experience: divine reality, the encounter, the sharing of life with God – luminous, sure, and strong.

Christ, so very present and concrete to us – one of us – is at the same time the One Beyond who resolves the enigma of existence. Christ is the meaning of history and the Lord of the universe, the viewpoint that explains everything. The experience of Pentecost constitutes the advent of a *Christian culture*, the definitive discovery of the "true light that enlightens all who come into this world."

The first gesture recorded in the Acts of the Apostles is the first great affirmation of this new culture, this new and definitive vision of reality "not revealed by flesh and blood, but by the Father who generates all things."[5] Immediately, and before peoples from all corners of the known earth, Peter announces the discovery of Christ as the cornerstone of God's plan. This is the unremitting cry of this awareness, the powerful testimony that spreads throughout the world and throughout history from the very first Christian sermon.

The entire human experience is illuminated by God's perspective. It is the tidings of truth's definitive criterion, the advent of the definitive culture.

THE EXPERIENCE OF THE GIFT

In the Liturgy, the communication of God's Spirit is called "Donum Dei Altissimi" (Gift of the Highest God). This is not a human construct, conquest, or even foresight, and even less a human right. It is a pure gift.

And so the Spirit of God is a pure event within us, a total surprise, an absolute gift that has only one analogy: the total gratuitousness of our being, our very existence. However, a bestowal whose meaning has not been revealed to us cannot be considered a gift. We could not recognize life and the universe as gifts if we did not await the revelation of their meaning.

Thus the Spirit of Pentecost is *the* gift *par excellence*, because it is through the Spirit that we are drawn into the mystery of Christ and understand the experiences of that person who fully explains and resolves our reality. "Faith is the light of the world." Human solitude dissolves with the advent of this gift. Human experience is no longer a lonely, disconsolate powerlessness but awareness and vitality, as the flame indicates the sign of the coming of the Spirit, "forcefully and gently."

The fearful darkness that the apostles experience is transformed into a courageous lucidity (note their confrontation with civil and religious authorities).

Existence becomes an immense certainty: "This is the victory over the world – our faith."[6] They are no longer alone; they experience the promise of Christ: "I shall not leave you orphans."[7]

Truly man is no longer alone, because by now the most authentic cry of the battle of existence is Saint Paul's: "There is nothing I cannot master with the help of the One who gives me strength."[8] We cannot strip ourselves of our weakness and of that which confines us. Rather, an Other accompanies us, "like a giant on the path." A new existence is realized. The irresistible impetus of God's presence mysteriously enters the fragile human makeup, at the source of this "new creature."[9] Our strength is an Other. Our certainty is an Other. Existence is a profound dialogue. Thus solitude is abolished at its very roots in every moment of life.

To exist is to be loved definitively ("He is faithful to his love")[10] and to abandon oneself definitively to this love ("Life to me, of course, is Christ").[11] Human existence is an inexhaustible, supremely powerful friendship.

THE NEW COMMUNITY

Solitude, as we have described it, draws us closer to others and allows us to share with them the experience of universal need. The resulting community offers the only experience of shelter, temporary relief, and fixed certainty for those who are lost and confused.

Our attempts to make up for all we feel we lack constitute a worrisome and anxious undertaking. The results are ambiguous and fragile, and each generation feels painfully pressed to denounce and alter them, when, as often happens, "the wrath of searching in vain"[12] compels us to reckless impatience and intolerance, bitter violence, and tragic presumptions. Human civilization thus creates communities with such precarious and deceptive patterns that they smack of snares rather than of steps on the true path.

Overcoming solitude in the experience of the Spirit of Christ not only draws us near to others but also opens us to others to the very depths of their being.

Our true life is Christ. Christ is the meaning of the existence of each one of us. Our life, the meaning of our existence, is summed up in, indeed is, one sole reality: "I am the vine and you are the branches."[13] The community becomes essential to each of us, to our lives. Human solidarity becomes the Church. "We" becomes the fullness of "I," the law of the I's fulfillment. "We have passed out of death and into life, and of this we can be sure because we love our brothers," writes Saint John to the early Christians.[14]

Such a unity, as absolutely unforeseen as it is indissoluble, makes the Church the redemption of the human community, the ideal of the community. "May they all be one. Father, may they be one in us, as you are in me and I am in you, so that the world may believe it was you who sent me."[15]

The certainty of the journey and the power of the Spirit of Life generate an untiring awareness in a given community ("For every unfounded word men will answer on Judgement Day")[16] and a ceaseless activity (meditate once again on the parable of the talents), with dedication to the death (the good shepherd gives his life for his flock). From the depths, a richness and intensity of works and a deep urgency impels the life of the community, which is born of the coming of the Spirit: "Before God and before Christ Jesus who is to be the judge of the living and the dead, I put this duty to you, in the name of His Appearing and His Kingdom: proclaim the message, and welcome or unwelcome, insist on it. Refute falsehood, correct error, call to obedience – but do all with patience and with the intention of teaching."[17] This vigilant passion for time, things, and people leads to a life shared (convivenza) among people and with the world around them. *The Christian community inevitably creates a new civilization.*

The more unerring the faithfulness to the Spirit of Christ, the more the paths of this civilization are experienced as ideal, definitive paths.

The encounter with any Christian community that seeks to live resolutely in the name of Christ inevitably attains a way to share life totally, an atmosphere, and such an unusual human rhythm that it cannot but strike the observer as something new, strange, and remarkable – a totally human ideal.

SOLE AUTHORITY

The supreme authority is the one in which we find the meaning of all our experience. Jesus Christ is this supreme authority, and it is His Spirit who makes us understand this, opens us up to faith in Him and His person.

"Just as the Father has sent me so do I send you."[18] The apostles and their successors (the Pope and the bishops) constitute, in history, the living continuation of the authority who is Christ. In their dynamic succession in history and their multiplication throughout the world, Christ's mystery is proposed ceaselessly, clarified without errors, defended without compromise. Therefore, they constitute the place, like a reliable and effervescent spring, where humanity can draw on the true meaning of its own existence, probing ever deeper.

What genius is to the cry of human need, what prophecy is to our cry of expectancy, so the apostles and their successors are to announcing the response. But just as the true answer is always perfectly specific and concrete with respect to the expectancy – which is inevitably vague and subject to illusions – so are they, like an absolute and reliable rock, infallible: "You are Peter and on this rock I shall build my Church."[19] Their authority not only constitutes the sure criterion for that vision of the universe and history that alone explains their (i.e., the universe's and history's) meaning; it is also vital – it steadfastly stimulates a true culture and persistently points to a total vision. It inexorably condemns any exaltation of the particular and idealization of the contingent; that is, it condemns all error and idolatry. The authority of the Pope and bishops, therefore, is the ultimate guide on the pilgrimage towards a genuine sharing of our lives [convivenza], towards a *true civilization*.

Where that authority is not vital and vigilant, or where it is under attack, the human pathway becomes complicated, ambiguous, and unstable; it veers towards disaster, even when on the exterior it seems powerful, flourishing, and astute, as is the case today. Where that authority is active and respected, the historic pilgrimage is confidently renewed with serenity; it is deep, genuinely human, even when the expressive methods and dynamics of sharing lives are roughshod and difficult. We must emphasize one important point: the gift of the Spirit manifested to the apostles conveys Christ's value as "The Way, the Truth, the Life." It gave the apostles a conscious and enlightened abandonment as the origin of their irresistible courage and vehement confidence in affirming their Master before the culture and civilization of their times.

Still today it is the gift of the Spirit that allows us to discover the profound meaning of Ecclesiastical Authority as a supreme directive on the human path. Here is the origin of that ultimate abandonment and of that conscious obedience to it – this is why it is not the locus of the Law but of Love. One cannot understand the experience of that definitive devotion that binds the "faithful" to Authority without taking into consideration the influence of the Spirit, and that devotion often affirms itself on the Cross of a mortification of the drive of our own genius or our plans for life.

From our brief meditation we can also say that without the gift of the Spirit we do not know how to recognize the teachers of the true civilization, and humanity does not find the strength and wisdom to build a common, balanced, and enlightened unitary path.

OUR FATHER

The unexpected gift of the Spirit renews us, and the supreme fruit of this renewal is our capacity for a new word and a new gesture that express the way we feel, face, and engage ourselves with reality.

The urgency of human needs and the inexhaustible attempts to satisfy them, the inevitable and intolerable final perplexity – all of this inspires, shapes, and continually stirs up a human cry for a committed human gesture, which our nature demands. Such a cry and commitment may be expressed uncertainly and vaguely but, if guided by violence, may also take on the morbid incomprehension of madness. The human person knows not what he or she reaches out to and awaits. The gift of the Spirit and the discovery and acceptance of Christ as the centre of all things finally give definitive terms to man's commitment to word and action, endow him with an awareness that fulfills reason's thrust and a promise of complete freedom, which is a specific, unambiguous goal.

The new cry, "the redeemed word," is *Christian prayer*. "For when we cannot choose words in order to pray properly, the Spirit Himself expresses our plea ... and makes us cry out, 'Abba, Father.'"[20]

Saint Paul's observation recalls the wonderful human and Christian document that is the first part of the eleventh chapter of Saint Luke:

Now once He was in a certain place praying, and when He had finished one of His disciples said, "Lord, teach us to pray, just as John taught his disciples." He said this to them, "Say this when you pray:

Father, may thy name be held holy,
Thy kingdom come;
give us each day our daily bread,
and forgive us our sins,

for we ourselves forgive each one who is in debt to us.
And do not put us to the test."

He also said to them, "Suppose one of you has a friend and goes to him in the middle of the night to say, 'My friend, lend me three loaves, because a friend of mine on his travels has just arrived at my house and I have nothing to offer him'; and the man answers from inside the house, 'Do not bother me. The door is bolted now, and my children and I are in bed; I cannot get up to give it to you.' I tell you, if the man does not get up and give it him for friendship's sake, persistence will be enough to make him get up and give his friend all he wants.

"So I say to you: Ask, and it will be given to you; search, and you will find; knock, and the door will be opened to you. For the one who asks always receives; the one who searches always finds; the one who knocks will always have the door opened to him. What father among you would hand his son a stone when he asked for bread? Or hand him a snake instead of a fish? Or hand him a scorpion if he asked for an egg? If you then, who are evil, know how to give your children what is good, how much more will the heavenly Father give the Holy Spirit to those who ask Him!"[21]

Our aspirations are translated into a deeply personal "you," as particular and familiar as a mother, and into a very clear, exhaustive plea, an awareness of the relationship between the two participants in the dialogue: "Our Father … thy Kingdom come … forgive us our sins … free us from evil … No one can say: Lord Jesus, if not in the Spirit."[22] And the redemption of the gesture is the *Sacrament*. With the Sacrament the existential commitment no longer runs the great danger of losing control, of veering from the path to true reality by falling prey to the appearance of things. In the act of the Sacrament, the visible sign that engages the human person leads him or her to touch divine reality with an indescribable confidence. Thus no human action meets so serenely and comprehensively that expectancy that calls man to action.

There is a marvellous consequence of this redemption of the human word and act: the communital dimension emerges from the very heart of the new word and gesture of prayer and the Sacrament. There can no longer be a true pleading with God or a commitment to Him that is not, at least implicitly, open to the entire community of His Kingdom. The openness to the community determines the truth of the word and the rightness of the act. "When you will pray, you will pray like this: Our Father, thy kingdom come ... We form a single body because we all have a share in this one loaf."[23]

On our common path our inability to be happy is the most powerful motive to share our lives; but, much more profoundly, it leads us to discover that each individual's happiness is a Reality common to all; one thing: "one Spirit, one Lord ... one God."[24]

The Liturgy is the greatest expression of the freshness of prayer and action with which the Spirit imbues us. Liturgy generates the supreme form of the earthly community, where the individual is enhanced in all his aspects by accepting the universal communion of the children of God. Here, even the material world – time and things – is assumed in a sole gesture that truly represents the beginning of the redemption of that same physical nature to which Saint Paul refers: "From the beginning till now the entire creation, as we know, has been groaning in one great act of giving birth."[25]

Because of its completeness the Liturgy becomes the unique locus of a genuine, complete education in receiving the Spirit and following His transforming power.

4 The Christian Existence

Only in clarity and confidence can we find the energy to act.

The event of the Spirit overturned the apostles' faint-heartedness and inspired the most intense, courageous, and dynamic adventure that the history of the human spirit has known.

"You alone, Lord, make me rest secure."[1] The discovery of Christ as the centre of all things eliminates fear and makes us sense a capacity to "possess" everything we encounter: "all are your servants, but you belong to Christ and Christ belongs to God."[2]

More precisely, this new culture demands an extremely rich concept of life: unremitting activity, unavoidable responsibility, a true "service" in every moment, every word ("whether you are eating or drinking"[3]); service to the *Kingdom*, that is, to that plan of the universe by which Christ heads all of reality. Everyone's existence has a meaning, which is to say that one truly exists insofar as one is in the service (a part of the whole, a "function") of Christ's Kingdom, a function foreseen by the Ideal Himself who established the mysterious plan for all things. And *consciousness* is such insofar as it is aware that it is destined to a task, and this awareness is the encounter between God and the individual – the event of the *vocation*.

That encounter occurs fully in Christ. Everyone's vocation takes place within the ambit of the personal and mysterious reality of Christ: "You have been created in Christ Jesus."[4]

To become aware of one's own vocation, to understand one's life by following the calling, to conceive of one's existence as in service to everything: here is the vital commitment of one's very being which Christ's Spirit plainly demands, giving one the strength to begin and to remain faithful.

The modern conception of life never shows itself so far from the Spirit of Christ as in the whole question of vocation. Today's mentality accustoms us to look to the future with a criterion focused on profit, enjoyment, and comfort. The road to choose, the person to love, the profession to undertake, the faculty or department in which to enrol – everything is determined by the criterion of absolute utility for the individual. And this seems so obvious and taken for granted that the shock of the provocation seems to be a challenge to common sense, an infatuation, an exaggeration, even to many persons of integrity. These accusations are also heard among educators who conceive of themselves as Christians or parents who are worried about the worldly success of their children. Judgments in public and private life, advice for the good life, warnings and corrections – everything is dictated by a point of view in which the total devotion to, and preoccupation with, the Kingdom is completely absent, in which the reality of Christ is missing. "How can I make the world work to my advantage? How can I get the most out of everything and everyone?" – these are the criteria dictated by collective wisdom and pragmatism.

The Christian mentality overturns, contradicts, and represses those questions, forcing the exact opposite to the fore: "How can I give myself as I am, serve all things, the Kingdom, and Christ evermore?" This is the only educative criterion for the human personality as redeemed by the light and strength of the Spirit of Christ.

Simple, lucid, comprehensive sincerity and resolute magnanimity as a Christian concept of our own existence can develop easily and surely only in early youth.

The profound availability of our complete life to the service of all things is also extremely important for understanding *what* it is we are called to carry out, *for understanding our personal vocation.* What I must do, what I must be – my vocation – does not normally emerge as a specific command, but as a suggestion, a proposal, an invitation. Vocation, which is the meaning of one's life, introduces itself more as a glimpse of a possibility than as something absolutely inevitable. The more difficult the task to be accomplished the truer this is. In its purest and most evocative aspect, awareness is the most discreet cue: it is inspiration. Thus one confirms one's personal worth by readily agreeing to the subtlest of possibilities.

CHARITY

To accept life as vocation, as service to (a function of) the Whole, is to define existence as a profound destiny to *share* Reality (of which we are born and on which we continually depend) and to participate in Reality, accepting it and offering ourselves to it as to the will of God, to His Kingdom. To accept life as vocation engages our existence as *charity* (*caritas*).

Let us point out the most exceptional paradigms of love's richness and simplicity, at the origins of the new humanity redeemed by the Spirit of Christ: "May they be so completely one."[5]

and they had the apostles called in, gave orders for them to be flogged, warned them not to speak in the name of Jesus and released them. And so they left the presence of the Sanhedrin glad to have had the honour of suffering humiliation for the sake of the name. They preached every day both in the Temple and in private houses, and their proclamation of the Good News of Christ Jesus was never interrupted.[6]

As I said before, let no one take me for a fool; but if you must, then treat me as a fool and let me do a little boasting of my own … Hebrews – my enemies – are they? So am I. Israelites? So am I. Descendants of Abraham? So am I. The servants of Christ? I must be mad to say this, but so am I, and more than they: more because I have worked harder, I have been sent to prison more often, and whipped so many times more, often almost to death. Five times I had the thirty-nine lashes from the Jews; three times I have been beaten with sticks; once I was stoned; three times I have been shipwrecked and once adrift in the open sea for a night and a day. Constantly travelling, I have been in danger from rivers and in danger from brigands, in danger from my own people and in danger from pagans; in danger in the towns; in danger in the open country, danger at sea and danger from so-called brothers. I have worked and laboured, often without sleep; I have been hungry and thirsty and often starving; I have been in the cold without clothes. And to leave out much more, there is my daily preoccupation: my anxiety, for all the churches. When any man has had scruples, I have had scruples with him; when any man is made to fall I am tortured. If I am to boast, then let me boast of my own feebleness. The God and Father of the Lord Jesus – bless him forever – knows that I am not lying. When I was in Damascus, the Ethnarch of King Aretas put guards around the city to catch me, and I had to be let down over the wall in a hamper, through a window in order to escape.[7]

The first apostles truly *followed* the Master, who was describing his own soul in the parable of the Good Shepherd, where charity reveals its deep need for initiative, creativity, and vigour. "Who among you with a hundred sheep, losing one, would not leave the ninety-nine in the wilderness and go after the missing one till he found it? And when he found it would he not joyfully take it on his shoulders and then when he got home, call together his friends and neighbours? 'Rejoice with me,' he would say, 'I have found my sheep that was lost.'"[8]

UNIVERSALITY

The very nature of Christian action, that is, to share, unquestionably demonstrates its boundless domain: a commitment to a genuine experience of charity signifies a complete openness towards the universe. All limitations to the breadth of our existence imposed from within suppress love. Love is not a matter of taste or measure, nor is it some intelligent plan of ours. It is a humble clinging to being as it offers itself to us. Hence the essential characteristic and the ultimate test of the Christian existence is its boundless openness, that is, its universality.

Even an authentically human attitude necessarily reaches out to everyone because humanity inevitably belongs to everyone. Attention to one's own experience is not authentic if separated – even unwittingly – from everyone else's experience. However, the clarity of a universal perspective and the energy to follow it in practice are more a gift than a conquest, more an encounter than a personal brilliance or intelligence: they are the fruit of the Spirit.

And so we understand why the first action of the apostles after Pentecost, Peter's speech to the Hebrews, bears witness to such a spirited and unambiguous devotion to a boundless ideal. The Church came of age as soon as the Lord's command, "Go therefore and make disciples of all the nations,"[9] became an overwhelming and concrete reality through the Gift of the Spirit. Indeed we move from childhood into adulthood only when we begin to walk towards the universal.

A particularly human act, a fruitful work, is realized, for at last it has been brought back to its original dimensions.

No existence that does not emulate this simple openness to the universe is Christian. This openness does not manifest itself in an impossible contempt of, or inhumane disinterest for, the particular, but in the way in which the detail is lived. We may commit and genuinely dedicate ourselves to family or friendship, class or school, studies or profession, but *the motive behind the commitment* must transcend any particular desire for a higher mark or attachment to a particular person. It must not dwell on detail, however important. It is easy to enjoy or justify becoming involved with our immediate surroundings; however, any choice that has no other motivation but itself is only inflated selfishness, misguided sentimentality. Unfortunately, the modern attitude eloquently affirms – even in the pompous lies of its boastful universalisms – its incapacity to venture beyond a limited perspective, and soon proves itself utterly incapable of fidelity to the particular, which becomes perceived as petty and as narrow as a prison.

On the contrary, only the confident freedom of a Christian existence, its vigilant detachment from all particularism, its resolute readiness for any authentic freshness constitutes a sure promise, a prophecy of the coming of the Kingdom.

See what days are coming – it is the Lord Yahweh who speaks –
days when I will bring famine on the country,
a famine not of bread, a drought not of water,
but of hearing the word of Yahweh.
They will stagger from sea to sea,
wander from north to east,
seeking the word of Yahweh
and failing to find it.
That day, delicate girl and stalwart youth shall faint from thirst.[10]

NOTES

CHAPTER ONE

1 Acts 1:6.

CHAPTER TWO

1 John 1:35–9.
2 *See* John 1:45–9.
3 John 2:11.
4 *See* Matthew 9:1–8.
5 Mark 5:32ff.
6 Matthew 8:23–7.
7 *See* John 4:1–30.
8 Luke 19:1–18.
9 Matthew 22:15–22.
10 John 8:2–9.
11 John 7:45–6.
12 Luke 9:47.
13 Luke 7:11–15.
14 *See* Karl Adam, *Christ Our Brother*. New York: Collier Books 1931, chapter 1.
15 *Essenza del cristianesimo*. Brescia: Morcelliana 1993.
16 *See* John 6:67–9.
17 John 10:30.
18 *See* Acts 1:6.
19 Matthew 16:13, 15, 16, 17ff.
20 John 8:12.
21 2 Peter 1:19.
22 Luke 24:28–32.

CHAPTER THREE

1 *See* John 16:12–13.
2 1 Corinthians 2:11.
3 Romans 8:9.
4 *See* Acts 2:14.
5 Matthew 16:17.
6 1 John 5:4.

7 John 14:18.

8 Philippians 4:13.

9 2 Corinthians 5:1; Galatians 6:15.

10 2 Chronicles 5:13.

11 Philippians 1:21.

12 Giovanni Pascoli, "Il libro," in *Primo poemetti*. Bologna: Zanichelli 1904.

13 John 15:5.

14 1 John 3:14.

15 John 17:21.

16 Matthew 12:36.

17 2 Timothy 4:1–2.

18 *See* John 20:21.

19 Matthew 16:17ff.

20 Romans 8:26, 15.

21 Luke 11:1–13.

22 1 Corinthians 12:3.

23 1 Corinthians 10:17.

24 Ephesians 4:5, 6.

25 Romans 8:22.

CHAPTER FOUR

1 Psalms 4:8.

2 1 Corinthians 3:22–3.

3 1 Corinthians 10:31.

4 Ephesians 2:10.

5 John 17:23.

6 Acts 5:40–2.

7 2 Corinthians 11:16–33.

8 Luke 15:4–6.

9 Matthew 28:19.

10 Amos 8:11–13.

Notes on the Christian Method

To the Pope of *Ecclesiam Suam*
As the expression of the meditated and faithful
endeavour of his students in Milan

1 A Great Premise

I Saint Paul wrote to the early Christians in Corinth that he had based his message "not on arguments based on human reason ... so that your faith not be founded on the wisdom of men, but on the power of God."[1]

Christianity is not born as the fruit of our culture or as the discovery of our intelligence. Christianity does not communicate itself to the world as the fruit of modern or effective initiatives. Christianity is born and spreads throughout the world through the presence of the "power of God:"[2] "God, in your name, save me."

God's power reveals itself in facts, *events*, which constitute a new reality in the world, a living reality; in movement, and thus in an exceptional and unforeseeable chronicle within the history of humanity and things.

Christian reality is God's mystery that has entered the world as a human history. Only God's power, no matter where, starts, spreads, and guides Christianity in an individual and in society. Jesus Christ is the fundamental expression of that power. Thus only the reality of Jesus Christ converts a person's mind and heart.

Here therefore is the important question: how does the reality of Jesus Christ reach us? It is in answering this question that we authentically determine the reality of the Christian mystery. The reality of Jesus Christ is not reduced to the limits of His body and the ambit of His human actions. The divine power within Him allows Him to assimilate mysteriously but genuinely those people who bind themselves to Him. His personality extends itself by invading time and space and assimilating the persons and things that the Father places on the path to His mysterious maturity; this is the very basis of being. The complete reality of Jesus Christ is this "Mystical Body," as Saint Paul calls it, or "the Church," as it is known in history. It is through the latter that Jesus Christ reaches men and women and generates in them a new outlook and life: hence we speak of "Holy Mother the Church." The spread of Christianity in the world takes place through the presence of the mystery of the Church, which coincides with the face of Christ at every particular moment of history.

The Kingdom of God, Christian Reality, is born and communicates itself *in any* setting in the measure to which the Church is present in that milieu. This presence finds its authenticity insofar as it is the instrument through which God's power communicates the Christian message and generates conviction and conversion. The supreme rule of the Christian method is to make the Church present in a given setting. The fruit of this presence will then depend on the "timing" or circumstances chosen by the mystery of God.

II What makes the Church present methodologically in a given setting?

1 *Unity expressed visibly* by Christians (see John 17).

At the very least this expression implies participation in the Sacraments; however, in the measure to which they are consciously lived, the Sacraments tend to generate an altogether communital structure of life, of all of life, from the way one conceives of one's existence and that of the world, to the way in which one ponders events, plans the future, approaches work, manipulates reality, and in particular, uses one's own means. The Sacraments, if lived with awareness, require a conception of life as communion. They reveal unity in Christ as the deepest truth of the same personal I, and they unleash from the depths of this I a desire to express that unity visibly and to spread it socially as the greatest good for the order of the world and for the person's road to happiness. "All of us are one thing only that partakes of the same bread."[3] In each setting there is thus a new life, a new and visible reality ("that they might see your good works"[4]) whose motivation and value can be verified.

2 *The link to authority,* that is, to the bishop; in Saint Ignatius's words, "united with the bishop as with Christ."

This is the "form" of every true Christian community, the factor that ensures its authenticity, its integration into the mystery of the Mystical Body, and thus also its participation in that redeeming power. Consequently, we can say that the Christian community in a given setting constitutes Christ's presence and thus the presence of the divine power that gives birth to His Kingdom and extends it insofar as it is guaranteed by, and founded in reference to, authority; insofar as it is a "mission" and lived as such. Everything must be profoundly subordinated from its very origin to that point of reference and, if needs be, sacrificed. It is through authority that the energy of the mystery emerges. That energy is not born of the shrewdness of our psychological and pedagogical conceptions nor of our social experiments.

A witness in a given setting is only authentically Christian insofar as it has two factors at heart. Even if a Christian is isolated in particular surroundings, all of his or her life there must look to the birth of the Christian community; a Christian's presence must be animated by the awareness of the mission that has been explicitly or implicitly generated in him or her by the bishop.

Even the most astute or generous social dynamism, open cultural expression, or dignified moral stance are ambiguous testimonies if not qualified by those two factors; that is, visibly expressed unity and the link to authority. Only through them, do these expressions inevitably and openly attribute their value to Christian Reality as objective Reality, as something concrete that transcends them. Otherwise observers will all too easily identify the value of a witness with the specific person who accomplishes it, and will ascribe this achievement to an exceptional group or a modern movement with praiseworthy personalities and their own determined ideas. The less upright the observers' intentions, the more unthinkingly will they admire, befriend, or follow a group or person. Everything will remain at the level of "opinion" and the decisive criterion will always be of their choosing, whereas the drama of conversion is to feel oneself called back to an objective Truth, beyond any person, and to acknowledge the concrete presence of a reality that is Christ's mystery in history, in the Church.

Without an immanent and expressed reference to the community and authority, a testimony can easily be reduced in the heart of an observer to an example of gentlemanly conduct, modernity of spirit, or social sensitivity; that is, to an idea or a way of life and not to a *reality* outside ourselves; to the "glory" of man and not of God, to another form of man's kingdom, not the Kingdom of God.

The method of spreading the Christian tidings and education must take its cue from that principle and from these concrete conditions and seek to embody all that they imply and suggest.

2 The Encounter

1 How wonderful to reflect that even in natural time the divine Power calls men and women to assume their place in the providential plan through the phenomenon of the *encounter*! While one aspect of the world is governed by a mechanical system, such that we are able to intuit and discover its laws, the more typically human aspect, where freedom, intuition, and love come into play, is completely evoked by this sequence of apparently chance encounters. This is almost irrational and is not translatable into laws. And yet this is precisely what creates human history within the evolution of the universe.

The word "encounter" implies, first, something unexpected and surprising. Second, it implies something real, that really touches us, is of interest to our lives. Understood in that way, every encounter is unique and its determining circumstances will never again be repeated because each encounter is a particular example of the "voice that calls each one by name." Every encounter is a great opportunity offered to our freedom by God's mystery.

In the history of God's kingdom the initial revelatory event is an encounter. In the Old Testament a voice calls a person in a specific location: "God placed Abraham to the test and said to him: Abraham, Abraham, and he answered: 'Here I am.'"[1] But what wonder and sweetness – in Mary as in us – to hear the Great Voice heard by Abraham, Isaac, Jacob, Moses, and Jeremiah become the presence of Gabriel: "Hail Mary."

However, all of this was a premise to the even more unexpected, shocking, sweet, and unique Encounter, the Great Occasion of human history. Let us read the chronicle of that first day in which it began to become clear (John 1:35–51). If we read the Gospel it still seems as if we take part in the very beginnings of the Kingdom of God through Christ's *encounters*: the encounter with the paralytic (Matthew 9:1–17); the encounter with Matthew (Matthew 9:9); the encounter with Jairus's daughter and the woman with a haemorrhage (Matthew 9:18–26); the encounter with the two blind men (Matthew 9:27–31); the encounter with the possessed mute (Matthew 9:32–34); the encounter with the rich young man (Matthew 19:16–22); the encounter with the widow of Nain (Luke 9:11–17); the encounter with the centurion (Luke 7:1–10); the encounter with the penitent woman (Luke 7:36–50); the encounter with Zacchaeus (Luke 19:1–10); the encounter with Nicodemus (John 3:1–11); the encounter with the Samaritan (John 4:1–42).

And finally, the instrument of the burgeoning of God's kingdom in the Roman Empire, Paul, was captivated in the memorable encounter that seems to unite the mysterious form of the Ancient Voice with the concrete humanity of a companionship: "Saul, Saul, why do you persecute me?"[2]

2 At the origin of the history of Christianity we find simple people who encountered someone and followed Him. But how can we, now, after two thousand years encounter Jesus Christ? Let us return to this fundamental problem, which we have already outlined in the premise.

As a child grows into adulthood and alters his or her way of living, his or her face and appearance may change; yet we are dealing with the same person. Thus the manner, visage, exterior appearance in which the reality of Jesus Christ introduces itself to us two thousand years later differs from the way in which that same reality appeared to the first disciples. From the very beginning the way to make contact with Him was not only to see Him in the flesh; there was also another way: to listen to His disciples.[3] Christ's figure in human history introduces itself with the face and appearance of those persons who follow Him, the face and appearance of the Christian Community: "Saul, Saul, why do you persecute me?"[4]

The community of the Church is the visage that the reality of Christ takes on in our life. Christ was truly man. He was hungry and thirsty. At times He was so tired as to sleep in a boat tossed about by a storm. And He truly died. Analogously, we make up the Church: we who eat, suffer, die, and are so human that the first Sacrament of our journey is Penance.

The encounter with the Church is the encounter with an objective reality, with a physically perceptible fact that is not any less real than the encounter with mother, father, family, or friends.

We can have ideas and opinions that originate in Christian truth, but they are still not the redeeming Christian life. We are called to adhere to and participate in a reality that comes from outside ourselves: the community in which Christ places us.

This community, made up of men and women like us, has spread to every part of the world. God communicates Himself to us through this human reality. This is the value of the Church:

"I am not asking you to remove them from the world, but to protect them from the evil one … as you sent me into the world I have sent them into the world … I pray not only for these, but for those also who through their words will believe in me. May they all be one. Father, may they be one in us, as you are in me and I am in you, so *that the world may believe it was you who sent me.*"[5]

Thus, the instrument of the world's conversion is the visible unity of the Christian community. Through it God's mystery once again proposes itself to the individual and society.

To rebuild the experience of God in this world within our own existence we must live the experience of the Christian community, that is, the Church. We are called to live the experience of the Community that Christ left in this world, which leaps across the centuries without interruption, reaching men and women, calling them, in the same way that He reached us.

3 The Christian community makes the Church present in a given place, either provisionally or permanently, depending on what the place itself requires and authority decides. The Church is not primarily an institution or association: it is above all a life, a new and surprising life for the "world."

Jesus Christ was the concrete, physical type of this new humanity. He was so much like others that people would ask one another what it was He wanted. When He spoke He used the words and ideas of His people. And yet it was another world that He revealed, one certainly not foreign to the human person. The hearts and the eyes of the people, previously unaware of this world, sensed their birth before them and within. Jesus said to Nicodemus "Verily, verily, I tell you, unless a man is born from above, he cannot see the kingdom of heaven."[6] Christianity is a new way to live in this world. It is a new life. Above all, it does not represent a few particular experiences, ways of doing things, additional gestures, or expressions or words to add to our usual vocabulary. The Christian uses the same vocabulary as others but the meaning of the words is different. The Christian looks at all of reality in the same way as a non-Christian, but that which reality tells him or her is different and he or she reacts in a different way.

What characterizes a Christian is a profound loyalty to his or her surroundings, because the place that God has entrusted to him or her is within this world, with its joys and toil; that is, in "what surrounds him or her." However, the Christian faces this small part of the world, clings to it, with a new heart and spirit born "not out of human stock, or urge of the flesh, or will of man, but of God himself."[7]

Certainly, we are always tempted to become bogged down in the skepticism of Nicodemus: "But how can that be possible?"[8] The answer is discovered only in the experience of the life that the Christian community calls us to fulfill, by continuously renewing the fresh awareness of early Christianity as is witnessed by this ancient passage, the Letter to Diognetus:

For Christians are distinguished from others neither by country, nor language, nor the customs which they observe. For they neither inhabit cities of their own, nor employ a peculiar form of speech, nor lead a life which is marked out by any singularity ... they display to us their wonderful and confessedly striking way of life. They dwell in their own countries, but simply as sojourners. As citizens, they share in all things with others, and yet endure all things as if foreigners. Every foreign land is to them as their native country, and every land of their birth as a land of strangers. They marry, as do all others; they beget children; but they do not destroy their offspring. They have a common table, but not a common bed. They are in the flesh, but they do not live after the flesh. They pass their days on earth, but they are citizens of heaven. They obey the prescribed laws, and at the same time surpass the laws by their lives ... They are poor, yet make many rich; they are in lack of all things, and yet abound in all ... they are reviled, and bless; insulted, and repay the insult with honour; they do good, yet are punished as evil-doers. When punished, they rejoice as if quickened into life ... what the soul is in the body, that are Christians in the world ... the world also hates the Christians, though in nowise injured, because they abjure pleasures ... Christians are confined in the world as in a prison, and yet they are the preservers of the world ... God has assigned them this illustrious position, which it were unlawful for them to forsake.

4 Everyone can see that encounters in the past and present are at the origin of a truer participation in the life of the Church and thus of the community. Therefore, each one of us can become an "encounter" for companions and friends.

To understand the value of all this we will address our attention to the following issues among many possible ones:

a. Our encounter with a vital Christian community or a Christian who is striking because he or she says something to us that we feel to be true, has an incomparable newness, freshness, and value. However, we can encounter a tradition, which has its roots in the centuries, within our present reality through a phrase, a word, or a gesture. This is to say that the encounter with that community or that friend brings us tidings that spring from a life lived through the centuries, through *tradition*. Each of us emerges from a stream that is born of this human and Christian solidarity. Thus, to love the community and the encounter that has generated it means to love this tradition of which we are born, to acknowledge this age-old reality that makes possible the Christian existence within us. Only our commitment to tradition, to the Christian reality through the centuries, can make us capable of being an encounter for others in our turn, of representing for others as well that unexpected freshness that recalls the origin of our being.

Therefore, the experience of the encounter is an experience of freshness whose depth is proportional to our awareness of its being rooted in a long history. We must thus educate ourselves to love this past life that has moved through the centuries to reach us with the visage of our life today.

b. Just as we have not arranged the encounter, neither are our actions conditioned by our success. The motive that moves us and justifies our extending outward is not within ourselves but at our depths, where we find an Other, Him whom we adore. We do not wish to form a party or faction or our own program. We wish to realize something that is other, pure, pristine, that does not depend on us but on the One who made us.

For this reason, if the encounter is accepted simply, it gives us a great freedom of spirit that never hinders us but allows us to act independently of our cultural attainment or shrewdness and even beyond our heart. We have this faith and confidence because an Other acts within us. Our freedom is that simplicity and naïveté that allows us to never tire of turning to whomever, of extending once again to whomever the invitation to that definitive encounter in the life of a human being.

c. The encounter with God or a person or the community can spring from the evidence of a moment and then be lived only as a memory. At times it seems like "a beacon in the fog," but still this fleeting appearance leaves us with the confidence of having discovered "something that has something within."

Even if darkness closes in on us a moment later, we will no longer be the same. A possibly indifferent disposition on our part can only reflect a state of the heart that tries to suppress the memory of that encounter; but that encounter remains an indelible fact in our life. In any case the encounter will be more meaningful insofar as we introduce ourselves to it without preconceptions, conditions to impose, or plans to approve, but with profound openness. This is the only disposition that corresponds to that sense of mystery from which every human comparison with reality should begin.

This openness is called "poverty of spirit" in the Gospels, and it is also "freedom of the spirit."

THE ENCOUNTER AS VERIFICATION

1 An encounter that does not beckon us is not genuine. Every appeal is always objectively a *proposal*. The more intelligent and sensitive one is the more one sees how much one's life is threaded by encounters and how each encounter constitutes a call and contains a proposal. In the immense panoply of proposals that constitutes the web of our existence, we are urged by nature to "compare" immediately each proposal with that complex of original structures – principles, evidences, needs – that constitute our being. If in this comparison the proposal that is made to us seems to answer our authentic needs, if it appears to enhance our possibilities, then we are automatically attracted to it and accept

it. Saint Augustine spoke of a "delectatio victrix," a conquering pleasure or attraction. The psychological game that he indicated, however, can be understood as inherent in Saint Thomas's definition of truth: "adequatio rei et intellectus," that is, the discovery of a correspondence between what is placed before me (the "proposal") and what I am aware of as being the structure of my nature. That is to say, the call implies the proposal of a truth so existential, of something so pertinent to our nature and life, that we feel compelled to try to understand where it is taking us: we feel motivated to adhere to it.

This interior process, which characterizes the life of every reasonable being, even though it becomes lucid self-awareness only in the philosopher, is at the origin of the immediate reaction of all those people who met Jesus: "This man certainly speaks with authority – He has done all things well; He makes the deaf hear and the dumb speak – There has never been anybody who has spoken as he has – powerful in the things He said and did in the sight of God and of the whole people."[9] Besides, Jesus had foreseen this: "Still happier those who hear the word of God and keep it." The encounter with the word and power of God is always an encounter with something that reveals one to oneself; that empowers , enhances one. It was like that from the great hope raised in Abraham: "Look up to heaven and count the stars if you can: such will be your descendants"; to the great task to which Moses was called: "So come, I send you to Pharaoh to bring the sons of Israel, my people, out of Egypt"; to the great, tragic fascination that bound Jeremiah to his mission.[10]

The Psalms, however, express the same thing for everyone: "How happy those who respect your decrees – Repeat oh Lord the word on which you have built my hope – Had you not been my consolation, I should have perished in my sufferings – Place in my heart a deep joy, greater than an abundance of corn and wine."[11] Peter's expression in the Synagogue of Capernaum is the simplest yet most powerful example of the call and proposal immanent in the encounter with Christ, and of its force, which compels adherence to Him: "Lord, to whom shall we go? Only you have the message of eternal life,"[12] the words that give meaning and value to our lives.

It should be noted that only those who continuously followed and sincerely committed themselves to Jesus felt the strength of that proposal in all its intensity.

2 Today, the Christian proposal, like the encounter, is identified with the call to us from a human reality surrounding us; and it is magnificent that this unique proposal among all others should have such a concrete, existential face, that it should be a community in the world, a world in the world, a different reality within reality; and not different because it has different interests but because of the different way in which it pursues common interests. The face of this proposal changes, but it remains one, the one mystery of the visible Church, of visible Reality. We must live this Reality, commit ourselves wholly to it; that is, enter it and compare all its movements, motives, and directives with the ultimate needs of our humanity. And insofar as we discover that those suggestions, those directives, those initiatives respond to our authentic human needs and help us to understand them, our adherence and conviction will be deep and definitive. So it is not a matter of studying theology or forming a group, it involves everything, all of life, because the proposal comes to us and meets us as *a new life*. To be "convinced" means that the totality of our "I" is bound to something: thus shall we all be bound to that Reality. That Reality will become us and we shall sense that we are that Reality.

One experience sums up everything that we discover in our Christian commitment: the awareness of being enhanced as a person, as an individual, while at the same time being in solidarity with the universe, a loving participant in the cosmos, enhanced in our personal authenticity and task in the world.

One is reminded of Christ's phrase: "He who follows me will have eternal life and the hundred-fold here."[13] The Christian proposal appears to us as a community which invites us to live a life: "come and see." We may almost have the same temptation as did Nicodemus to object: "How can that be possible?" But the response does not change: "Come and see"; that is, "follow me and you shall see." Even if this commitment is a "hypothetical work plan," we can say it implies that we enter wholeheartedly into the community of the Church, identifying the life of the community of the Church with our own life. Thus "we see"; that is, we become aware of what it is for us.

A true "verification" must be carried out. Whoever does not undergo this verification process will remain a Christian, but have nothing new to say, or else will simply leave.

3 An encounter that would not be a calling or a proposal to be verified would be so empty that one would not even recall it as an encounter; it would be so pointless as not even to belong to history. Each of us shall be a true and "historic" encounter for friends only inasmuch as his or her presence constitutes for others a specific call to Christianity and a clear proposal of the Christian community.

It is worthwhile to stress a few points regarding the humble and practical fact of the encounter, on which the attractive force of the Christian community in a given setting depends:

a. Above all, *we* are continuously the objects of Christ's calling and of the community's proposal. Let us remember what we would remind others.

A mechanical attachment to a certain position, as if it were almost a party line, is not the verification of a calling; a merely curious attitude is even less so; and yet less so is a spirit bent on accusing and judging possible faults; nor can we call frequent, material, external, passive participation a verification.

To verify we must *commit* ourselves completely, with a clear and renewed concentration. We must say the following about two aspects of this sincerity:

– The characteristics of a commitment to a given proposal are those that the proposal itself demands. We ourselves cannot determine how we shall carry out the verification. If the calling and the Christian proposal are to a life of community, then the community must determine the forms of that commitment.

– We are called to an experience that must be fulfilled with faithfulness, that is, for as long as the proposal is made to us. Verification is not authentic even at the beginning if we are not prepared to pursue our commitment for as long as required. We are called to pursue it to the end because the Christian proposal is made to us up to the last moment. The very nature of the Christian proposal demands this, because it is a calling to the mystery of God revealed in human history and thus a calling to our salvation. Only if we neglect our most basic human needs will we not take the Christian proposal seriously. There is no getting away from that calling: either adherence, which establishes its own drama, that of commitment and holiness; or the *search*, just as loaded with consequences. The true, genuine human attitude of those who know that they do not make themselves is to search for their own origins and destiny. Thus, even when they have not been able to "discover," they must feel that it is opportune and necessary for their lives to continue to verify the proposal. Even if one walks without seeing, one saves oneself by following, as "he who saw and touched." For this reason one who truly searches and one who has sincerely found have an unexpected affinity.

b. The Christian's proposal to others must be *authentic*. Let us note here some important aspects of this authenticity:

– We must clarify our concept of proposal so that no confusion lies in us – and the least possible in others – between proposal and propaganda. Propaganda is to spread something simply because it is one's own idea or because it is of personal interest. The calling, instead, as the Church understands it, is to awaken something that is already in the other, to enhance and value the other, as a gesture of charity. I appeal to my companions to help them find their truth, their true names (in the biblical sense), to find themselves. My Christian appeal is thus the strongest contribution to one's freedom, because freedom means to be oneself. For that reason our calling is the supreme gesture of friendship.

Above all, we are never called to determined forms, criteria, or schemes, or to particular organizations, but rather to that promise that constitutes the human heart. We repeat what God placed in others' hearts as He created them, placing them in a given setting, shaping them. For this very reason we do not know where God will lead them, perhaps even using our words as an instrument: the plan is His. We cannot know what their vocation will be.

Ours, therefore, is above all a calling to that which constitutes the value of a human life, to a destiny, a vocation, its fulfillment and nothing else.

– In proposing to the other we relive the motives for which we appeal to him or her.

It is exactly that splendour, the expression of this "reliving" of ours, that constitutes the calling to the other. Thus, the call is not something extrinsic to us, almost like a task outside ourselves. Once our adherence is no longer vital, our appeal becomes automatic, as if we were expounding a formula or ideology. Such an appeal is usually propaganda, which only generates arguments, making us feel estranged from others.

We must do things in such a way that everything – the initiatives that we undertake, the invitations we extend – is pervaded and animated by a genuine concern for the ideal. We have the same concerns as others, because they are human preoccupations. But we have something else: our every gesture is underpinned by the profound desire to love the person, that is, to help him or her to be truly free, to walk towards his or her destiny. This is the law of charity: the desire that the others be themselves, that they "save" themselves, just as Christ desired.

Like others, we want to go to school or work, we worry about achieving a good grade or a fair wage, we have a curiosity about things and events and a desire to have relationships that fill time and avoid boredom. But, above all, we want to be people who, beyond attending school, going to work, or being with friends, always strive for the ideal, the supreme ideal, Christ and the Church.

c. Christian reality calls us much more to a path than to a point of arrival. Above all, we must consider that we are beings on the path. We cannot start from the anguished effort to convert ourselves based on our own strength. We must keep this in mind even with regard to others, otherwise we will ultimately be disappointed – either with ourselves, because we shall always have our shortcomings, despite our commitment to our encounters; or with others, because they do not change as we would want them to; or with the subtle humiliation of seeing those whom we have called become better than us.

THE ENCOUNTER AS GRACE

1 "What is mortal man, why do you remember him, the son of Adam, that you should care for him?"[14]

"Moses said to God: 'But who am I?'"[15]

"And I said: Oh Lord Yahweh, look, I am not even capable of speaking; I am but a child!"[16]

"Lord, I am not worthy to have you under my roof ..."[17]

The purest and most objective value of Christian life is the awareness of the absolute gratuitousness of God's interventions in history, because there is no greater, sweeter, and more exalting truth. The encounters, which He created to make men and women – us! – part of His kingdom, are a pure gift that our nature would not have been able even to imagine or foresee. They are a pure gift above and beyond any capacity of our life. They are "Grace."

In His Mystical Body, Jesus Christ takes up again this entire Kingdom of "Grace," of the supernatural goodness of God's power. Just as Jesus of Nazareth's existence among the Jews and the possibility of encountering Him were grace for them two thousand years ago, so are the Church's existence in the world and the encounter with her in society grace for us today.

Not only the encounter but also the capacity to understand that calling is a gift of Grace.

"Blessed are you, Simon son of Jonah! Because it was not flesh or blood that revealed it to you but my Father who is in heaven."[18]

At that time, Jesus exclaimed, "I bless you Father, Lord of heaven and of earth, for hiding these things from the learned and the clever and revealing them to mere children. Yes, Father, for that is what it pleased you to do. Everything has been entrusted to me by my Father; and no one knows the Son except the Father, just as no one knows the Father except the Son and those to whom the Son chooses to reveal Him ..." "Because," he replied, "the mysteries of the Kingdom of heaven are revealed to you, but they are not revealed to them."[19]

And the capacity to verify this call, to recognize its value, is a gift of Grace. "I shall ask the Father and He will give you another Advocate to be with you forever, that Spirit of truth whom the world can never receive since it neither sees nor knows Him; but you shall know Him because He shall be with you and He shall be in you."[20]

"But the Advocate, the Holy Spirit, whom the Father will send in my name, will teach you everything and remind you of all I have said to you."[21]

"I have made your name known to the men you took from the world to give me. They were yours and you gave them to me, and they have kept your word. Now at least they know that all you have given me comes indeed from you."[22]

"The Spirit himself bears witness to our spirit that we are children of God."[23]

And the capacity to adhere to and fulfill the Christian proposal is a gift of Grace:

I am the true vine and my father is the vinedresser. Every branch in me that bears no fruit He cuts away, and every branch that does bear fruit He prunes to make it bear even more. You are pruned already, by means of the word that I have spoken to you. Make your home in me as I make mine in you. As a branch cannot bear fruit all by itself, but must remain part of the vine, neither can you unless you remain in me. I am the vine, you are the branches. Whoever remains in me and I in Him bears fruit in plenty; for cut off from me you can do nothing.[24]

After saying this, Jesus raised his eyes to heaven and said:

Father, the hour has come: glorify your Son so that your Son may glorify you; and, through the power over all mankind that you have given Him, let Him give eternal life to all those you have entrusted to Him. And eternal life is this: to know you, the only true God, and Jesus Christ whom you have sent.[25]

I have made your name known to them and will continue to make it known, so that the love with which you loved me may be in them, and so that I may be in them.[26]

Our minds and hearts are never commensurate with the steps that God takes towards us. The same supernatural goodness that makes the mystery of God assume the "form of a servant and the figure of man" (Saint Paul) in Christ and in the Church, also enables our spirit and sensitivity to understand these wonders. Otherwise they would remain like light for the blind or words for the deaf, like ultrasound that remains silent to our ears.

Thus even the encounter with that small part of the Church that is the Christian community in our particular environment is "Grace," a gift of God's power. And we need Grace to understand the call of those who belong to that community and guide it, to commit ourselves to verify their call and to hold faithfully to their proposal.

2 At this point we can understand what constitutes the expression of a true availability and commitment to the Christian calling: it is the attitude of asking, of prayer. The norm of the Christian encounter

immediately makes a sincere person aware of the disproportion between his or her strengths and the very terms of the proposal, of how exceptional is the problem posed by such a message. The most elementary aspect of our natural religiosity is the sense of our own original dependence. It disposes the simple soul to acknowledge that all the initiative may come from God's mystery and that the ultimate attitude to assume is the humble attitude of one who asks to see, understand, and adhere. This attitude of prayer is so fundamental that it belongs as much to those who do not as yet believe as to believers. It belongs as much to the Unnamed One in Alessandro Manzoni's *The Betrothed*, who cries out, "God, if you exist reveal yourself to me"[27] as to Peter, who exclaims "I do have faith, Lord, but increase the little faith I have."[28]

An availability before and a commitment to the Christian fact that do not translate into a plea, into "prayer," are not sufficiently true, because they do not take into account, with conscious faithfulness the meaning of the proposal that we are called to verify: "The hour is coming when anyone who kills you will think that he is doing a holy duty of God. They will do these things because they have never known either the Father or myself."[29] Our consciousness begins to participate in the mystery of the One who creates us at the point of pleading and prayer. And our spirit thus feels the awe of this Mystery that makes everything, absolutely everything, when it considers that even this initial activity of asking and praying is made possible only by a gift of the Creator: "No one can say, Lord Jesus, if not in the Holy Spirit. The Spirit comes to help us in our weakness, for we know not even what to ask for in prayer, nor how to ask it. But the Spirit Himself expresses our plea in a way that could never be put into words."[30]

The Liturgy of the Church educates us to look at God's ineffably profound initiative on our behalf when it makes us say: "Lord, you who inspire our desires by *anticipating* them, deign to accompany them with your aid."

Even the encounter with and the commitment to the most humble Christian community, in a given setting with everyday people, is not free of impurity that alters judgments and relationships, if it is not welcomed with that humble, active, vigilant availability of the heart that is the genuine impetus of prayer, albeit embryonic, vague, and confused.

THE ENCOUNTER AS EXPERIENCE

Experience is a fundamental method through which nature facilitates the development of awareness and the growth of a person. Thus we cannot speak of experience without an awareness of "growing" in it. However, to truly grow we need to be provoked or helped by something different from ourselves, by something *objective*, by something that we "encounter."

Only through a true, objective experience can men and women became aware of the presence of God in the world. Saint John writes about it forcefully to the first Christians: "That life was made visible: we saw it and we are giving our testimony, telling you of eternal life which was with the Father and has been made visible to us."[31] The presence of Christ in His Church becomes manifest through a true, objective experience in the life of one who lives with awareness.

Even the encounter with the Christian community or the verification of its message, as we have described it, is a true, objective experience. This Christian and ecclesial experience is vital and emerges from a three-fold factor:

a. The encounter with an objective fact, in its origin independent of the person who fulfills the experience; a fact whose existential reality is a visible community in the same way that any humanity that is wholly human is visible; a community in whom the human voice of authority with its judgments and directives establishes its criterion and form. Any version of the Christian experience, no matter how personal, must at least imply this encounter with the community and reference to authority.

b. The *power to perceive* adequately the meaning of that encounter. The value of the fact we encounter transcends the perceptions of human awareness and requires a gesture of God to be adequately understood. The same gesture with which God makes Himself present to the human person in the Christian event also exalts the cognitive capacity of awareness. It makes the acumen of the human gaze commensurate with the exceptional reality that attracts it. We call it the "grace of faith."

c. The *awareness of the correspondence* between the meaning of the fact that we happen upon and the meaning of our own existence, between Christian and ecclesial Reality and one's own person, between the encounter and one's own destiny: the awareness of this correspondence verifies that self-development that is essential to the phenomenon of experience.

As in any authentic experience, but above all in the Christian experience, it is patently clear that our self-awareness and critical capacity (the capacity to verify) are engaged and that an authentic experience is far from a simple impression and cannot be reduced to a sentimental effect.

In this "verification" the mystery of the divine initiative existentially enhances human "reason" in the Christian experience.

In this "verification" human "freedom" shows its nature. We cannot acknowledge the close correspondence between the present mystery and our own dynamism as human beings if not by the measure in which we accept our fundamental dependence, the essential fact of our "being made." This present and profound acceptance consists of simplicity, "purity of heart," and "poverty of spirit." All the drama of freedom lies in this "poverty of spirit" and it is so profound that normally it comes upon us unawares.

3 Communion

1 Why does God allow himself to be encountered in the world by means of His Church?

To have us enter His life, which is the foundation of all things. In Christian language this sharing is called *communion*, a beautiful word: "What we have seen and heard we announce to you, so that you too may be in communion with us. Our communion is with the Father and His Son Jesus Christ."[1]

"Communion" means a capacity for personal life so deep that a person cannot realise it alone: this capacity lies at the origins of our being, where it is made by God (significantly this is called "capacity for obedience"); it is the capacity to participate in the very life of the mystery that makes all things, the Trinity. By its nature, therefore, it is an irresistible force with which, little by little, God unites with Himself those whom He chooses according to His mysterious freedom.

This irresistible force of unity begins with Christ and permeates all the vagaries of history. "The Father has put everything in His hands." More precisely, it is a force that springs from His death and resurrection. So essentially it is *a communion with Christ*: "Everything I have received from my Father I have given to you."

This communion with Christ permeates the whole of life, generates new realities and therefore new dynamics in the whole of life and all of its various aspects: "All of us who were baptised in Christ were baptised into His death. For with baptism we were buried with Him in death, so that, as Christ was raised from death by the glorious power of the Father, we too might live a new life."[2]

This creates not only an invisible and spiritual unity but also a true physical one, like the unity of those who ate with Him, or walked with Him, or followed Him: the reality in which this complete communion with Christ is generated is the unfailing continuity of the Church community. Baptism and the other Sacraments are the moments in which all this is physically generated and regenerated.

2 But – and this is what we want to emphasize – by the very fact that we come into communion with Christ we come into communion irresistibly with all those whom "the Father has put into His hands"; in other words, with all those who, whether or not they are aware of it, have been seized by the mystery of Death and Resurrection in baptism.

This is why the communion amongst Christians in their particular environment, the unity they live together, which embraces all aspects of their presence in that environment, is the true irreplaceable witness to the living Christ, to the active power of His death and resurrection: "Christ yesterday, today, and forever." It is not true communion with Christ if it does not tend to become a Church community in a person's own environment. Communion with Christ is an eminently *personal* event; but the more conscious and faithful it is, the more it tends to generate a Christian community life, a moment of the Mystical Body in a particular place, and to identify the life of the individual with the life of that concrete community.

So in a given environment the mystery of divine and human Communion is present insofar as:

– there are Christians who acknowledge and practise unity of life amongst themselves as the expression of the most substantial reality of their own persons – an expression that is more deeply valuable and decisive than any other interest: "Life, for me, is Christ," and this Christ, more me than myself, is Christ in His Mystical Body; in concrete terms, therefore, the Christ of the community that touches me.

– such a unity of life is approved by the Bishop, and is maintained almost as a "hunger" for obedience to the Bishop, because – as we have said before – dependence on the Bishop ensures integration of the concrete community into the mystery of the Mystical Body.

On the other hand, the mystery of Christ and the universal Church is lived out through the concrete community in a particular place or environment, otherwise it would be transcendence without time or space, without incarnation. The power of Communion, proper to the mystery of Christ, reaches the individual and transforms him or her specifically through the reality of communities in the environment: there it meets the individual, regenerates him or her to a new outlook and inspires him or her to a new life. A community in a given environment is therefore the contingent aspect of the Community as a whole, but it is *de facto* the primary concrete instrument of life, albeit humble and provisional.

Not to understand the value of the community in the environment is to conceive of communion with Christ Himself and His Church in an abstract way. Not to love the community in the environment means to fail that communion and therefore to weaken or even make an illusion of Christian metanoia.

On the other hand, the vitality of the Church's spirit in any age is measured by the formation of many communities, each carefully tended to, in the environment, the practical point where people encounter the Incarnate Mystery; and by the intensity of their self-awareness and creativity, as well as their loving obedience to the Bishop.

We can usefully recall what we mean by "environment" or "surroundings." The environment is, in concrete terms, that complex of realities in which the individual is more or less firmly entrenched, which helps his or her development and shapes his or her personality in various ways.

The passion for communion that marks Christian consciousness must prepare us to identify the environments that most influence a society's individuals and to spread the Church's life there. Environments identified in this way vary from one period to another or even from one place to another: it would show a remarkable lack of Christian spirit and charity to favour certain forms that proved to be successful in the past over others, to the extent of sacrificing the flexibility – and freedom! – required to address the needs of new situations.

So communities in a given environment may have been fundamental in the past and remain fundamental today. In the past they may have been adequate to the task, whereas today they may not be able to manage alone, and simply to become fully alive, or to revive, they need communion with other incarnations of the Church community.

3 Obviously the community in a given environment does not live in isolation from other communities where that essential part of the Church's life that springs from the Bishop is expressed.

In their turn, the various communities in the environment live in communion amongst themselves, centred on the Bishop, just as all the Bishops live in communion among themselves, "founded" on the ultimate "rock," the Pope.

As it happens the word "communion" was used historically to mean this unity amongst the various Christian communities as the evident sign of communion of the mystery of God with man.

Every Christian and every single local community (which today are the dioceses and the parishes) knew that it was not the Catholic Church (the Church of God in Jerusalem, in Corinth, in Rome, etc.), except insofar as it remained in communion with all the other persons or communities, members of the Church. And all knew that only by keeping in contact with the vital network of the Church as a whole could one fully be God's witness in one's place, in one's surroundings, and therefore bear an infinite wealth. It is well known that these tight bonds and this intensity of life, contacts, and exchanges between the early communities did not close Christians in on themselves. On the contrary, this was the age of rapid and prodigious expansion.

The most recent studies show that first the apostles and then their successors, the bishops, long resisted the tendency to multiply local communities out of their desire to preserve true unity in the Church. Thus at first many cities, or dioceses if we can call them such, remained linked to an apostle; then for a long time the dioceses remained wholly centred around the bishop, and the "parishes" – in the modern sense – were few at first. It was only in feudal times that the number of parishes increased; and the clergy remained bound to their own Church, and to their own piece of land ("benefice") rather than to the bishop. One of the spiritual consequences of this was a weakened sense of ecclesial communion and contact with the life of the universal Church. This in turn led to a decadence of the clergy, who tended to isolate themselves and settle for the very limited religious needs of the people.

It is worthwhile to read the following note from Church history, to understand better how supernatural "communion" with the mystery of God needs to be expressed socially in the Church.

Unity in the early Church: Communion

When the Pope today solemnly sends an Encyclical Letter to the whole of Christianity he begins it with these words, "To all Patriarchs, archbishops, etc.; in *peace and communion* with the Apostolic See." *Peace and Communion* are not just words that appear continually in early Christian literature, but they indicate a concept that merits consideration as one of the keys for understanding the spirit of the early Church. Communion in the sense used by the early Christians is the community of the faithful, of the faithful with their bishop, of the bishops with their fellow-bishops, and all with Christ the head. The visible sign and at the same time the cause by which this community is continually renewed is the Eucharist, the sacrament of "communion." The sinner is excluded from eucharistic communion and, for this reason from the eucharistic community. A stranger who comes from a distant Church is admitted to communion if he presents a letter of credence from his own bishop proving his belonging to an orthodox community; otherwise he is refused the Eucharist and hospitality.

When at the end of the second century the bishop Polycarp went to Rome to discuss the question of the date of Easter, he could not reach agreement with the Pope, Anicetus; all the same, as Irenaeus was later to write to Pope Victor, "Anicetus granted him the Eucharist in the Church," which means that he allowed him to celebrate Mass in the Roman community and to administer Communion to the clergy and the people; "and thus they parted in peace." By this Irenaeus means that even though they had different opinions, the ecclesiastic community between them, the peace and communion, did not change. Here we see clearly that peace has a meaning quite distinct from that of concordance of opinions or the absence of differences. Peace and Communion mean a real bond that is not necessarily broken because of a dispute, and the sign of this real bond is the common celebration of the Eucharist.

In Rome, where the presbyters who were living alone in the suburbs did not celebrate with the bishop, but who, at least on Sundays offered the sacrifice of the Mass in their titular Churches, the custom continued that the bishop, who celebrated before all the others, would send an "acolyte" to take a piece of the consecrated host which the presbyter would place in the chalice during his own celebration. This custom is recalled in the mass today by the rite that follows the Kiss of Peace, accompanied by the words "Haec Commixtio et consecratio ..." Pope Innocent explained this practice thus, "So that [the presbyters] on this special day may not feel separated from our communion."

In ancient times "being in communion" with heretics meant to receive their Eucharist. This gave origin to the custom of lay people, who went off on a journey that would take them through regions where there was no Catholic Church, carrying the Eucharist with them, so as not to be obliged to take communion in a heretical Church, which would have meant associating themselves with that community.

When a Christian set off on a journey he would receive a letter of recommendation from his bishop, a sort of safe-conduct, in virtue of which he would be given a friendly welcome and hospitality in the community of believers. This institution, which dates back to Apostolic times, was not of advantage only to lay people, for example Christian traders, but to bishops themselves. They could, at little cost, send messengers and letters to all parts of the Empire. This is the only way we can explain the enormous correspondence that the prelates kept up between themselves. These safe-conducts were recognised by the name "Letters of Communion" (*Litterae Communionis*) or "Letters of Peace," as they attested that the traveller belonged to the community and as such could receive the Eucharist.

Ludwig Hertling[3]

4 Every Christian community is primarily a place of education for its members, because communion with the Mystery of God is something very great in which man must be continually reminded, adapted, and developed: "erunt omnes docibiles Dei," they will all be taught by God. That mysterious communion is a life, a life that must be continually made to grow.

Revelation has a fundamental rule for educating man in salvation in the Christian community: *"Follow me."* No other road, no intellectual power or shrewdness has the value of this rule: "You search the scriptures because you think you can get eternal life from them: and the same scriptures speak in my favour. Yet you do not want *to come to me so as to have life.*"[4] To go to Christ in order to have life is not to construct arguments, but to live the community through which He calls us. Only through this means can we verify the Christian proposal and come to realise that the end of all things is truly the Kingdom of God: "Since the world in its wisdom did not know God, it pleased God in his wisdom to save believers through the folly of preaching."[5] To try to manage alone, to attempt as it were to call God's proposals before the tribunal of autonomous criteria would be the most blatant vanity: it would be the sin of Lucifer, who claimed to give meaning to himself.

The Church's behaviour is a revealing confirmation of this great rule. The Church obliges us to only one thing each week: Sunday Mass. It would seem the least personal of all the Church's actions, but it is through this "doing as others do" that the Church guides us to God. After all, the framework of the Church's daily prayer, the Divine Office, is Psalm 119, which is a call to follow the "law," God Himself: "They are happy whose life is blameless, who follow God's law! … I have more understanding than the old, since I ponder your precepts."[6]

Saint Paul uses the word *obedience* to express the idea of following. Obedience means to abandon yourself to follow an Other, and obedience is the only true sacrifice, because sacrifice for the Christian is not necessarily pain or denying yourself something, but rather identifying your own will with that of an Other, of God. And it is exactly this law of obedience that makes us great and happy, and gives us "the hundredfold, now, in this world."[7]

In every Christian community established authority is the function of leadership, which prolongs the mission of Christ as Head. This is true for the realization of the Christian community at every level. The spirit of intelligent, faithful obedience to authority marks the depth and stability of "communion" in a Christian community.

On the other hand, God is quite free in choosing the ways He inspires and works wonders: He is able to draw true praise even from the mouths of babes, and can make the young wiser than the old, because the "Spirit blows where it will." It will therefore be the task of the authority, who is the first to live "communion," to be able to value all the freely given, unforeseeable blossoming of the Spirit's gifts in the community. But even a charism "edifies" a community only insofar as it is lived in communion with the institutional authority.

To follow does not mean to copy mechanically. Following is a human phenomenon, lived in your person, and the forces that distinguish your person are intelligence and will. Thus without a committed intelligence and freedom there is no true *following*. Therefore:

– following is not an unintelligent, unconscious attitude. Following must be a heartfelt effort to identify with the motives of what is proposed to us, to understand the values implicit in the suggestions offered us. By following with open eyes, with lively attention, we understand and learn; in other words we grow in spirit.
– following does not mean being carried along by the tide; rather it is a personal decision, a continuous act of personal freedom. For this reason Christian tradition advises us to say morning prayers every day, so as to take up again the conscious decision to follow God. "Blessed are those who follow the ways of the Lord," we say at midday prayer.

If you limit yourself to a passive obedience it is not true obedience. Obedience requires the compliance of our entire self, with all our faculties.

A DECISIVE COMMUNITY IN THE ENVIRONMENT

1 There is a natural phase in a person's life in which the education of his or her awareness and will is as acutely and radically vital as birth is to life: it is the moment in which the individual's "surroundings" become a whole new network of relationships with the "world"; new in its vastness, awareness, and initial true freedom. This environment obviously does not coincide with a "place" in the material sense of the word. More than a place, it is an ambit; in other words, a whole way of living, a web of conditions of existence.

Yet in present-day society this ambit of life pivots around a material, physical place, which becomes a kind of reference point or unavoidable crossroad for all those budding relationships, with their corresponding ideas and feelings.

Of course the phase of life we are thinking of is adolescence and youth. The places of reference are the school and, to a different extent, the workplace. These places lend their names to that environment so important for the whole of human life.

And these are the places that give their names to the Christian community that must become present in that environment. Just as adolescence and youth are the most decisive phases for the adequate formation of a person's awareness of life, so the Christian communities in the youth environment constitute an important educational instrument for the Church in that decisive phase.

2 Let us try to better grasp the meaning of these educative tools of the Church by taking a look at the social situation in which some of them arise.

From tradition to conviction. The culture we live in is saturated with the Christian tradition. Even the Church's opponents have this tradition immanent in the structures of their person, because they grow out of a soil that has been permeated with Christianity for two thousand years.

So we cannot avoid this tradition, which is such an intimate part of our nature, even though our spirit is free to renounce it. This is the tradition that our parents place us in by giving us birth: it is at our origin and at the basis of our education.

What must we do in order that this tradition not remain hidden in a dark corner of our consciousness, unexpressed and unclear in its meaning? What must we do in order that our life not come to an end without disclosing its most compelling aspect?

Tradition is given us like a seed that must mature and become identified with our whole person. It is through this very maturation that we take the step from unconsciously accepted "tradition" to "conviction."

At the first appearance of the critical spirit, the need to know and decide, the awareness of our own personality that is irreducible to any other, we need to experience the tradition that has been given us as something capable of making us live all aspects of life more deeply. We need to compare what our family and parish have given us with everything in our surroundings; in this comparison we try to see how Christianity operates. The discovery that Christianity makes us live things more completely and intensely helps to convince us that it is true, the true answer to our human nature.

We cannot be convinced about Christianity simply by studying it abstractly like some theory: we can be convinced only by comparing it with the whole of our life experience and ascertaining that it does answer all life's problems (and the more one grows the more these are relevant).

However, someone must help us to make this comparison at the time we need it most. There is a particular period in which people have the flexibility needed to make the ideological wealth of tradition a living experience. It begins at fourteen years of age, when the youngster opens up to a thousand interests and problems. If a young person is not helped in these years to understand how the Christian idea is able to clarify his or her interests and give a meaning to each of them, he or she will lose this opportunity, perhaps for good.

School and Christian education. In the Catholic conception of education, the school should be one of the principal instruments for verifying tradition against knowledge, to help people interpret, from a Christian point of view, the whole world that youth are called to enter.

A free school[8] is one in which the youngster is helped to test those values into which he or she was born.

This is the concept of the "pluralistic" school, which does not by any means connote a limited and closed development of consciousness, narrowed by blinkers; for it is only the mature awareness of one's own idea that can make one capable of true openness and dialogue, and therefore of true democracy. This is why we insist that Christian education must take priority over every other concern or commitment.

The school today. The school as it is today does not correspond[9] to this Christian conception of education. Even religion lessons remain a parenthesis, out of touch with the rest. The neutrality of present-day schools implies an "I couldn't care less" approach to the meaning of life and the ultimate sense of the topics under study. Students may be presented with a series of solutions, without having a true critical capacity with which to assess them. This type of education normally leads youth to develop a root of skepticism regarding all the more important human problems, if not an *a priori* refusal to take them into consideration; or else it ingrains in them a tendency to be hostile to their own original tradition.

Reform of the school structures falls within the purview of those who have certain responsibilities in society, and they will carry this out discreetly, in a calm dialogue. It is up to the student, with respect for democratic co-existence, to mobilize his or her spirit so that once an adult, he or she will be able to co-operate in bringing about situations more in keeping with Christian ideals. The youth must never be against the school and against teachers; however, he or she must perceive a need. It is a fact that, if a student is very committed to Christianity and to the Church's life, he or she will often be uncomfortable in the school. Teachers should not be prevented from saying what they think, but they should not use their teaching role as a means to attack the Church, a pretext to try to shatter the conscience of even a single youngster; they must be asked not to overstep the limits of their mandate as teachers.

If the school does not help in that work of comparison between tradition and the content of study, where can this help be found?

By means of a Christian structure generated by the free initiative of the persons concerned. This is the primary educative value of the Christian community in the school: to help carry out that comparison that the environment does not achieve.

So we can understand the importance of the young person's *free time;* by free time we mean all the space in which a person's initiative and creative commitment can express themselves according to the conscience and the will, unfettered by everyday commitments.

In this sense the more the value of freedom is safeguarded and fostered in social life, the greater the possibility that the Christian community flourishes in its surroundings. This freedom is gravely endangered when, for example, an attempt is made to turn "student associations" into official institutions, to make them effectively representative of the students as a whole, or "official" bodies of the school. These associations would extend the type of education we find in schools today and draw the students to the view of "throwing all ideas together and teaching democracy." The end result is a co-existence (or more often a head-on clash) among youth who are ideologically unprepared, and these associations end up being guided by non-Christian ideas, or even by various political propagandas that take advantage of ambiguity to assert themselves. Students who get into debates before shaping their own ideas are usually overcome, or remain conformist Catholics, or come to look at their faith as one idea amongst others, or defend it out of mere bigotry.

Youth need instead to deepen their own ideas in a qualified movement before politicizing their own position.

So we must leave space for this deepening, since only this can generate a maturity that will allow us to dialogue with others. What we want is a stable and valid democracy.

Christian students need a community that is tied to the destiny of the Christian tradition within them and in society and that offers itself as a locus for this commitment of their conscience, culture, and life.

This community therefore demands that they give it precedence in the use of their free time (already so scanty), and that scholastic institutions extend it exactly equal rights with all other forms of scholastic association. If they are based on an educational concern different from ours, then democratic freedom must be the same for all.

3 Let us look now at the place of these youth communities in the ambit of the broader Christian community, and clarify their relationship to the Church's main structures. These communities, remember, are meant to be an educative movement, an instrument to develop our Christianity intelligently and to mature our freedom. They are a temporary instrument, a provisional stretch of the road that we all must travel on the way to God's kingdom. The whole of a youngster's future life depends on the way he or she lives this phase. Certain things can only be learned in this period between the ages of fifteen and twenty years, when there is an openness and an intelligence regarding Christian life. Youth communities in the environment are therefore an extremely important instrument, but they are only one means and one phase in a much wider context. If we were to create our youth community today with the aim of remaining in this ambit forever, we would be proposing a stunted, closed ideal. We insist on our work today because it spurs us to prepare for tomorrow's work. Tomorrow each one of us will have a particular function in the Church; we will take up our road according to our own particular vocations, in our ambit and in keeping with our capacities, as many have done before. Therefore we must stress that while the community in the

environment is a very important instrument, it is only an instrument. This qualification draws attention to the limits of our task,
while at the same time it motivates us to use this enormous gift of
grace with all our hearts and strength. "You will be called to
account for every instant wasted."[10]

An instrument: but for whom and what? This instrument belongs
to the great life of the Church, to the mystery of God in the world;
and we are part of this mystery. So we do not feel the slightest
bit different from our friends who are in a seminary or convent
in Brazil, or who have set up house as a family. We are the very
same for we all belong to the mystery of God in the world, to the
Church. The Church is not the community in the environment;
the community in the environment belongs to the Church. It is an
instrument with which the Church forms us in our awareness of
the mystery of the Mystical Body of Christ.

Who governs the community of the universal Church, which is
so much greater than we are? Who can lead it authentically? Is it
someone better prepared in theology, perhaps, well educated or
clever? No. The one who leads this community according to the
mystery of God's wisdom is the authority: the bishops and the
Pope.

So the more the environmental community tries to be loyal to its
bishop, the more will it be an instrument that educates us in the
sense of the Church.

This will be the first condition for a movement to belong to the
Kingdom of God, and not to particular and limited ideas and
plans. If we abandon ourselves to our own criteria and measures,
we are not certain that we are educating ourselves in the Kingdom
of God, because the Kingdom of God is mystery, yet so concrete
that it is still crucified, crucified in those who belong to it.

A Christianity filtered by our wisdom, reduced to ourselves,
leads to ambiguity and not to witness. It generates compromise
with our opponents rather than the victory of our faith. We
cannot water down God's wine with the water of His opponents.
Christianity cannot be affirmed by toning down some aspects of
its truth. To love "others" does not mean to forget what distinguishes us from them so as to find points of agreement. We shall
not love others if we do not first of all offer them the reality for
which *we are not* like others; in other words, the reality that comes
from Christ.

But this new reality comes to us from Christ only in union with the bishop. This is why we must be loyal to the bishop, far beyond all diplomacy and subtlety; because only by following him can we be sure that we are bringing Christ to the world, and not some idea of our own.

Therefore the fundamental rule of our movement must be faithfulness and profound loyalty to our own bishop's way of thinking and his sensitivity. The Lord did not create some particular movement or association: he created bishops. Saint Ignatius of Antioch wrote, in one of his powerful, vivid epistles, that Christians must cleave to their bishop "as to Christ."[11] We belong to that one true universalism that is the Church only if we are bound to that father who generates us in the Christian life, to that man through whom alone passes the life that regenerates us: the bishop.

That authentic part of the universal Church that is proper to the bishop is called the "diocese." So the first directive of our movement must be profound integration into the life of the diocese. The bishops animate the life of their dioceses by entrusting individual areas to collaborators, the priests: thus the parish is born (from the Greek "para oichia," near home). Since the bishops insist on this structure, we must be deeply loyal to it and direct the outcome of our common work towards it.

But why does the Church place bishops and parish priests in each place? It does so because to educate people in Christianity the Christian voice must reach man *in his surroundings*. And the parish is the environment of families, which normally are basic for human life.

However, for the development of an individual, the "environment" is that locus of relationships that influences and determines his or her evolution the most, especially regarding outlook and sensitivity. Now, as we have already said, there is a period in young people's lives when what they see around them makes a stronger impression than what they were told at home as children. The home environment is still the original factor, but now other milieux influence them more: school, workplace, television, cinema, and other means of bringing people together. Our society uses these tools in a terribly invasive way, so that at a certain age the bond with home and with the parish is overpowered by a far more influential competition. Force of circumstance therefore leads the Church to its desire that youngsters be reached by the power of its help where the world, with all its collective means, penetrates minds and hearts more easily. So the Church community needs to be present and reach out in the very places frequented by youth of fifteen to twenty years of age: the school and the workplace.

As a rule the parish does not have a method that can contrast the influence of non-Christian social components in the school and work environments: this is the task and value of the student and worker communities.

The greatest problem of our age is to truly attend to and educate ourselves in the Church's appeal. Now, an action that aims to be educative must take into consideration the situation of the individual to be educated; in other words, it must be effected where he or she is more readily reached, most influenced, in the environments he or she frequents. To this end we need a flexibility of spirit capable of adapting tried and true methods and forms. "Man is not made for the law, but the law for man." Just as parents, knowing that their seventeen-year-old cannot be expected to behave as he did when he was seven, give him more freedom in the hope of maintaining a real contact with him, so does a parish at times need to show largesse in dealing with us, even though we are still bound to it.

The movement in the environment, then, is by no means in conflict with the original structure, the parish. Rather, it is meant to be the instrument that saves the Christian seed the parish germinates through a vital rediscovery of Christianity.

The more we grow in youth in faithfulness to the mystery of God in the world, the more, once we are grown up, will we take our place in the traditional structures. We repeat clearly to ourselves and to all that our concern is to integrate deeply into all the forms of Catholic life in our land. What generates and justifies our solidarity and our particular community today is the possibility and the reality of a proposal and of a more detailed and effective aid in educating youngsters in clarity, intensity, faithfulness, and Christian sacrifice. This is the community in the environment.

THE FIRST EXPRESSION OF COMMUNION: PRAYER

Every person has a basic religious attitude, because man is made to yearn for an all-embracing meaning of life. We cannot carry out a single action without implying – perhaps unawares, against our own theoretical convictions – the ultimate meaning of things. This affirming, perhaps unconsciously, of the ultimate meaning of life is called the *religious sense*, since it is born of the most elementary and impressive evidence that we can ever have: the evidence that the ultimate meaning is "more" than us, and that we depend on it totally. The religious sense of its very nature is the soul of all other interests, particularly because all our interests move us towards our happiness, our destiny; in other words, our ultimate meaning.

I am not the measure of all things: an Other is. So life consists in living for an Other, in affirming an Other. The Greeks used to speak of Fate; the Stoics of necessity; Christians speak of Providence. But over and above the differences, everyone has a clear awareness of this supremely evident reality: the fact that we depend.

Some actions tend to develop our sense of dependence, actions that express this awareness directly – since to express oneself is a law of nature.

The whole complex of these actions can be summed up in one comprehensive word: "prayer."

Prayer expresses the essential dynamism generated by the life of the Christian community, and through prayer the Spirit of communion penetrates and transforms our mentality (thus prayer is the first expression of obedience and so constitutes true "penance").

1 As the conscious expression of the religious sense, as we have already mentioned, prayer begins from our realization that we are not the makers of our own life, that an Other is the source of this life, freely, instant by instant. Birth is only the most striking sign of a permanent condition of the whole of existence: "We are made." That Source that is more me than myself, which I cannot think of without trembling and being attracted; this mystery, which makes me and is infinitely before me, is God.

Prayer acknowledges all this. And its best expression is "Our Father." "Tam Pater, nemo," "No one is such a Father," because if our father, in one moment, set off the process of our life, God makes us be continuously, and we are His infinitely more than we are our father's or our mother's. Saint Paul said, repeating the words of a Greek poet, Aratos: "In Him we live and move and have our being."[12] God is my root: "Our Father, who art in heaven"; in other words, in the depth of our being.

This brings us to a wonderful and revolutionary discovery: that we are continually wanted, in other words loved, by God; that to exist is to be loved by God.

2 But God's creative act makes man eternally intent on what in philosophical terms we call "perfection," and in psychological terms we call "happiness." God sets us on a road we cannot leave: so much so that to say "no" consciously to this irresistible dimension of our being leads us to that terrible breakdown that on earth is despair and in eternity, hell, the eternal refusal of a happiness made for us. This law of our being is so true that we do nothing, we remain psychologically inert, if we are not moved by this desire.

No true self-awareness, no true prayer occurs if it does not coincide with the entreaty to be more perfect and therefore happier.

Jesus suggested this prayer: "Our Father ... thy kingdom come, thy will be done." For our perfection and happiness are His Kingdom and His will.

One must be superficial and lacking in common sense to see prayer as a cowardly attitude or entreaty as weakness. To ask for perfection and happiness is a need implied in our nature, and since man is essentially dependent, any other attitude would be foolish presumption or empty pride.

Because the whole range of our actions constitutes our attempt to journey towards happiness, prayer, by reawakening our awareness of the true road to this happiness, must be aimed towards becoming a constant dimension of man in action. Jesus said, "Pray always."

3 For this same reason we must "multiply the gestures" of prayer, which, while not the full extent of our religious attitude, educate us in that mature gaze on all those things to which it aspires. Multiply the gestures, because a law of our soul is that only by multiplying actions do we assimilate their spirit.

Jesus Christ Himself created gestures of prayer that generate in man that communion with His mystery and therefore that participation in the mystery of God that is the aim of human history. These gestures are essentially Christ's actions in His mystical Body, therefore actions of His community as such and at the same time acts that constitute, create, the community. The Sacraments are the gestures through which Christ spreads His mystery in the world (the Sacraments are also called "Mysteries").

Through the Liturgy the Church gives these mysteries of Christ an educative value, extending them to fill man's whole day. This is the value of the Hours of the breviary (the Divine Office).

But the religious spirit finds or adapts so many forms of expression and nourishment: those more immediately contemplative (meditation); humbly repetitive ones (the Holy Rosary); or the impetuous or sweet kind, like a short cry of the heart (ejaculatory prayers).

4 Mission

MISSION

1 The mystery of God engages the whole universe, and its communion motivates us towards an unforeseeable unity of human reason. "Everything is yours, and you are Christ's and Christ is God's."[1]

Jesus Christ was *sent* to "take up all things" in Himself and so we are sure of all being one single thing: "there is no longer slave or freeman, Greek or barbarian, man or woman: we are all one in Jesus Christ."[2]

In history, though, this truth has not yet been wholly expressed and *realized*. This is why everyone who participates in the "communion" of the Church also participates in Christ's mission. This striving to embrace the whole world is in direct proportion to the truth of one's "communion" with Christ and the Church, and therefore of one's own Christianity. Thus this striving marks the truth or the intensity of "communion" in the Christian community.

The Church's missionary drive lies primarily in the power of its unity and the attraction that this arouses in any environment. Its impulse "to witness to the ends of the earth" comes more from within than from an exterior need or appeal. There is no doubt that the time has come to understand that, before talking of the damnation of "unbelievers," unless we live this missionary dimension, those who risk getting lost are first of all Christians themselves. "If the miracles worked among you had been worked in Tyre and Sidon, they would have made penance long ago in sackcloth and ashes."[3]

Whatever the case, as long as a person or a Christian community is not open to living communion with other Christians, and, through them, with all men, they deprive themselves of the opportunity of fulfilling their own personality, of being fully and authentically "Catholic." They impoverish themselves and reflect a paltry image of the "unfathomable riches" of the mystery of God.

We must insist, though, that universality is nothing less than that space destined for the communion that is the essence of Christianity and that generates itself in the individual through participation in the community of the Church. Universality is the spreading of communion among us. The proposal to "go as a missionary" is not a matter of insisting primarily on the particular needs in a certain environment (ignorance, poverty, etc.), but of becoming totally involved in the Christian community of the place, and therefore sharing in its hopes and needs. In this case, if one feels truly in "communion," vitally integrated into the local community, then being "strangers" from a human point of view will only make the universality of Christianity and the power of charity show themselves more plainly; charity creates a bond of total unity between persons whose different mentalities and nationalistic feelings would otherwise keep them divided and totally separated.

We should note that this missionary communion is also required to enrich the community of origin; that is, the home base of those who are sent to the missions. Their going away would be only a loss and impoverishment were it not to lead to a contact with the life of other members of the Church, to be the beginning of an exchange. The feeling of many, even of people in leadership, that "sending" some people abroad is a waste of energy is a serious symptom of the loss of the sense of Christianity as communion. To say, "There is a need here, why go there?" would not seem to correspond to a true Christian understanding.

2 Mission is the Christian's original mode of dialogue. Unity is definitive, not differences.

We can already begin to build unity, one step at a time, by entering into dialogue with others, with each person, in the hope that he or she may change. Respect for differences is not to be mistaken for the absence of hope that we can reach unity with the other person, that the other person can live our life, that the new life may reveal itself to everyone.

The proposal of unity must be tireless and patient in the devotion with which one attaches oneself to the person of the other.

The history of the Church is the history of the building up of unity, based on the capacity to recognize the positive value of dialogue. We have only to think of the encounter between Christianity and the various civilizations, of the wealth and attractiveness of the liturgical forms.

Everything is ready to be taken up by the Church. A youngster sent to Brazil by his community wrote, "I feel the need for an explicit Church, it's not enough for me to think of the Communion of Saints, or rather, it runs the risk of becoming an ethereal concept compared with the sea of people I meet on the streets every day. If history is not a farce, this reality asserts its expression as Church, its historical maturity as Church." The last assertion can be only the desire to see the Church expressed, a built-up unity that moves in history.

This active desire, therefore the "mission," begins with the life of the Christian community in its environment. The tireless dialogue with one's companions is born of the initial certainty of a common destiny that unites us and the desire to express true unity visibly in the environment. Certainly it will take patience, because this will be evident only in the end. But we must re-make the road towards unity with everyone, because we know that the other, too, is called to take up a place in this plan. And the dialogue will spread from its own environment to another person, then another, in a greater and greater circle of interests, towards a space of communion and an ever-wider ambit of charity: from your own school to the entire student world; from your own workplace to the whole world of work; from the city to the suburbs, to the countryside; from your region to one further away; from your own nation to others.

But the environment that suits our presence is the world. If the mission begins with the nearest surroundings, its tendency is universal: unity is not authentic if not open to everyone. The aim of mission is total unity. There is no reason for excluding anyone or anything: to discover the other means, at the outset, to discover all others. "I have made myself all things to all men."[4] So in every Christian community that has an authentic spirit, there are always at least a few who choose to repeat the gesture of God's Incarnation in a unique and exemplary way, to accept the sacrifice of being born again in another environment. The history of the Church's unity makes its way above all through these friends of ours. With them the whole community moves definitively towards the perspective of unity, because their presence in far-off lands is a reality. What happens in a far off land is, for those who remain in their community of origin, the prophecy of unity. And those who have gone live this prophecy within themselves. "We have become a miracle to ourselves," some of them have written. To follow the path they have shown us means to allow that unity to be born in us and our attitude and interests to be identified with those of the "Catholic" Church.

DEMOCRACY

Democracy is not only the condition for the social development of a missionary communion but also an initial expression of it.

1 The ideal of democracy normally arises as the need for well-defined, proper relationships between persons and groups. More particularly, the starting point for a true democracy is the natural human need for co-existence that may help the person to affirm himself or herself and for "social" relationships that do not obstruct the growth of the personality.

The principle of democracy is therefore the meaning of man "in his very being"; to consider, respect, and affirm man "because he is."

In its spirit, democracy is not primarily a social technique or a fixed mechanism of external relationships. There is a temptation to reduce democratic co-existence to mere external order or behaviour. When this happens respect for the other tends to become basic indifference.

The spirit of a genuine democracy instead moves each one to have an active respect for the other, in a correspondence that tends to affirm the other's values and freedom. The kind of interpersonal relationship that democracy tends to establish could be called "dialogue."

Dialogue as a method of co-existence is clearly and qualified by and rooted in an "ideology," in a certain way of conceiving of oneself, others and the world; the will for dialogue cannot be separated from one's sensitivity and conception of life.

Even the most sincere democrat is tempted to retain the wonder of his or her own conception of man and the world as the real criterion.

Now to make this not a hope but a motive and criterion for relationships is violence, the violence of an attempted triumph of an ideology that would eliminate the affirmation of the free individual. The effort, for example, to create "Socialist Internationals," or the impetus to level out everything at all costs by "leaving aside what divides us," can be moving as an inspiration, but in fact it always ends up crushing the person in the name of an ideal framework or a flag.

The criterion for human co-existence must affirm man "inasmuch as he is," and so the concrete ideal of earthly society will be to affirm a "communion" among the various ideologically engaged freedoms.

The contract that regulates life in society ("Constitution") must try to give ever more perfect norms that assure people of co-existence as communion and educate them accordingly.

2 Christians are particularly disposed and sensitive to this value, precisely because they are educated in affirming charity as the only law of existence; for this the ideal of every action is communion with the other and the affirmation of the other's reality "because he is."

But only in Christian charity does this affirmation find its true expression, since in Christian charity the ultimate motive for that respect for people is made clear. The ultimate motive cannot be only the fact that "a man is a man"; the ultimate motive of my respect for someone else must be something that concerns my origin and my destiny, my good, my salvation; it must be something that corresponds perfectly with my end: something that can enter into definitive communion with me.

The ultimate motive is the mystery of God, in His essence (Trinity) and in His historical manifestation (Kingdom of God). I must actively respect the other (love), because the other belongs to the mystery of the Kingdom of God; I must approach the other almost with the same religiosity with which I approach the Sacrament, because the other is a part of God's plan, and the mystery of God is a mystery of good that is beyond my control.

Without this basis, the affirmation of the person as the ultimate true criterion of social life cannot be sustained and nourished, but will collapse and once again become insidiously and violently ambiguous.

This is why Pius XI once said, "Democracy will be Christian or it will not be" (because, although God "can raise up children of Abraham even from stones," it is also true that the Church is where the awareness of His mystery lives).

3 A government of the *res publica* that draws inspiration from the Christian concept of co-existence will have pluralism as its ideal. In other words, the fabric of social life will render possible the existence and development of all efforts of human expression.

To realise this pluralistic co-existence implies grave problems: pluralism is an ideal directive for this world. We must, however, commit ourselves to it without fear.

Pluralism, inasmuch as it tends to affirm all particular free experiences in all their authenticity, is decidedly against a concept of democracy and openness that is espoused by a certain mentality prevalent among us. Relativists, whatever kind of relativism they live, provided they are relativists, tend to be called democratic; consequently anyone who affirms an absolute is identified as antidemocratic (intolerant, dogmatic).

This mentality, or any compromise with it, leads to the attempt to define as "open-spirited" those who are ready to "put aside what divides us and look only at what unites us," accepting a "setting aside of ideologies" (a "de-ideologization") laden with ambiguities.

In particular it is remarkable to see how such a position tends to deprive the Christian presence in the environment and society of its unique meaning, to empty the Christian presence of the content of its communion, to dissipate the very essence of its mission.

Above all we can easily observe that the first essential denied to Christians in the name of this false democracy is their communital presence in society: every manifestation of that essential fact, for which the Christian lives and acts in communion and obedience and therefore hierarchical communion, will be condemned as narrowness, integralism, or even clerical dictatorship.

For Christians, democracy is co-existence; in other words, the acknowledgment that one's life implies the existence of the other; and the instrument of this co-existence is dialogue. But dialogue is to propose to others what I am living and to take note of what others are living, out of respect for their humanity and out of love for them; it does not at all imply a doubt in oneself or a compromise.

Democracy, then, cannot be founded interiorly on a common ideology but only on charity; in other words, on human love, adequately motivated by man's relationship with God.

DIALOGUE

The instrument of co-existence with the whole of human reality made by God is dialogue. So dialogue is the instrument of *mission*. If we were to be totally cut off from the world, from others, alone, absolutely alone, we would not find any novelty. Newness always comes from an encounter with the other. It is the rule with which life is born: we exist because others have given us life. A seed left on its own does not grow; but placed in a setting where it can be nurtured by something else, it opens up. The "other" is essential for my existence to develop, for my vigour and life. Dialogue is this relationship with the "other," whoever and however he or she may be.

What does the other bring? Certainly, always a sphere of interest, which as such is partial, but in the network of ordered relation-ships helps to bring about a harmonious maturity, a completeness. Each one of us, because of one's particular temperament, tends to stress certain things; contact with others reminds one of other things and of other aspects of the same thing. Dialogue is thus a function of those horizons of universality and totality to which man is destined. Let us remember therefore the important function of dialogue for the Church's Catholicity.

Unlimited openness, which is appropriate to dialogue as the factor that makes a person evolve and creates a new society, has one serious prerequisite: it is never true dialogue unless one is truly aware of oneself. In other words, it is dialogue only if it is lived as a comparison of the other's proposal with one's own proposal; it is dialogue only insofar as one has a mature aware-ness of oneself. So if the "crisis," in the sense of being challenged to re-evaluate one's own tradition, does not logically precede the dialogue with the other, then either one will remain blocked by the other's influence or the other, whom one rejects, will provoke an irrational hardening of one's own position. Therefore dialogue implies an opening towards the other, whoever it is – because everyone witnesses an interest or an aspect that one may have set aside, and therefore anyone at all provokes one to an ever more complete comparison – but dialogue also implies a maturity, a critical awareness of oneself.

If we do not keep this in mind then a great danger emerges, that of *mistaking compromise for dialogue*. To take what we have in common with the other as a starting point does not at all mean saying the same thing, even if we use the same words: what is justice for another is not justice for a Christian, what is freedom for another is not freedom for a Christian; education in someone else's conception is not education as the Church conceives it. To borrow a term from scholastic philosophy, our words have a different "form"; we have a different form in our way of perceiving, feeling, tackling things. What we have in common with the other is to be sought not so much in ideology as in the other's native structure, in those human needs, in those original criteria, in which he or she is human like us. Openness to dialogue, therefore, means the ability to take as a starting point those problems to which the other's ideology or our Christianity proposes solutions, because what is common to different ideologies is the humanity of the men and women who carry those ideologies as banners of hope or as an answer.

5 Culture

Participation in the life of the Christian community brings about a new awareness of existence and reality: new not in the sense of different, but in the strong sense of the word, that is to say definitive – according to the expression of the Liturgy, "the old has passed away, all things are made new"; all the efforts made up to now have been completed, not through our initiative, and the meaning of reality is now revealed in a definitive way.

Christian culture therefore points to the definitive view on the whole question of our existence and the reality of the cosmos.

1 We can begin to understand the originality of Christian culture if we remember, even from the historical point of view, how it definitively intensified mankind's most authentic and impassioned efforts to reach a true "point of view" on reality, to achieve a culture.

Let us take the most significant example, the cultural effort that had an essential importance in the formation of Western civilization: Greek culture.

The Greeks conceived of culture as vitally connected to human existence: it was lived as an awareness of human life, an attempt to give definitive meaning to day-to-day events – good, bad, happy, painful, or transitory.

And from the beginning, reality, "aion" (that is to say firmly rooted in being and therefore not the work of man, but a "given"), was sensed to be "in communion," in a mysterious communion that human thought had to reveal and bring to light; hence the Greek term for truth, "aletheia," as reality to be led out of hiding.

Two concepts that Greek philosophical thought intuited were "cosmos" (order, harmony of all Being) and "dike" (justice, law, the profound rhythm of Being, consonance as opposed to discordance). These concepts point to the impact on Greek thought of the intuition of reality as communion. Impelled by this intuition, Greek thought went in search of the *other world*, that is to say the stable zone of being, the mysterious principle of communion of reality and mankind. The search for this dimension of reality (and if there is no seeking, said Socrates, man's life is not worth living, because man dies in day-to-day events if he does not grasp their genuine meaning) was conceived originally as "listening to" what that mysterious origin wants to say to man's desire.

The word "logos," which defined man's thought as capable of revealing truth, of bringing "aletheia" out of hiding and into the light of evidence, recalls existentially the concept of a self-fulfillment of Being that man's consciousness acknowledges.

In Greek philosophical thought, Platonism marked the grasping of a fundamental point. The world of ideas was the sphere from which the world of things of all times received its consistency and significance; and the relationship between the two worlds was defined, albeit tentatively, in a more precise way. The tangible world *imitated* the world of ideas, *participated* in the world of ideas. With the concept of "participation" a great light entered into Greek thought: the whole of reality, from its greatest and worthiest to its smallest and vilest aspects, constituted a great harmony, because it participated in an Other world. The whole of man's life should therefore be lived in the light of this participation: it became the principle of morality, the form of human co-existence. The most evocative witness to this passionate endeavour came from the Greek world.

Just as Greek thought passionately strove to achieve culture, so was it also acutely aware of the inherent limits to the vision it had formed. Thus all its cultural formulations harboured an awareness of these limits so sincere that they can only be a reminder and a lesson for us. The Greeks were aware that however complete the cultural vision they had formulated might be, Reality, Being, went immeasurably beyond, surpassed it in all directions. All of the

Greek philosophers' almost incredibly dispassionate self-criticism tended to measure the disproportion between Being and their own conception of Being. They were such genuine philosophers, in other words listeners to the voice of Being, as to be aware that their stumbling efforts interpreted that one Voice inadequately and therefore betrayed it.

This is why the word "certitude" was unknown to them. The greatest philosophers, once they reached the furthest step, confessed that all was re-consigned to Being, that all they had thought needed a confirmation that they themselves could not give. In sum, even their most ingenious formulations had to acknowledge the essential uncertainty of the thought of a single man.

2 "The Word was made flesh and dwelt among us." The Eternal entered into time: the truth finally became present without veils and without misgivings, no longer as the endpoint of a fierce longing, no longer as a hope that moves men to all kinds of different inventions, but as an irremovable concrete presence. A Man's voice, a Man's presence, a Man's life shared. Just as unforeseeably as at the creation, God's initiative answered mankind's fervid expectation. The truth came and filled our hearts. Man's thought is of value only if it adapts itself to His truth present among us. The world with all its measures, criteria of judgment, and action, "*jam iudicatus est*," has already been judged; a new logic surpasses the old in all directions, "Stumbling-block for the Jews, foolishness for the Gentiles."[1]

When He spoke of Himself and the new vision of man's and reality's existence that He founded, Jesus Christ used the word "rock": that which cannot be moved, which is the foundation of all things, without which nothing can be built, which takes away all uncertainty. Whoever met Him, having first lived the experience of the Greek culture, witnessed in a moving way that what the Greeks had sought and sensed, that unknown God to whom they had raised an altar in the Areopagus, had arrived. Now they had to abandon themselves in gratitude for the evidence of His presence.

"The Logos is not hidden from anyone, he is a common light, he shines for all men: for the Logos there are no Cimmerians, let us hasten towards salvation, towards rebirth."[2] Christ reveals the plan of reality to men: He is the origin, the one destiny of men and things, for Him a mystery of redemption of the whole of reality is realized. The "Communion" intuited by the Greeks finds in

Him its point of consistency: reality exists because it is communion with Him; man's life is true insofar as it becomes acknowledgment of communion with Him.

Thus Christ is shown as the principle of the definitive culture.

In him everything was created as its centre of unity, harmony, and cohesion that gives the world its meaning and value and through this its reality, or, to use another metaphor, as the place in which all the lines and all the generators of the universe tie together and coordinate themselves. Whoever establishes a point of view on the whole universe, past, present, and future, sees all beings ontologically hanging from Christ and becoming definitively intelligible through him ... Fixed in him, all things as it were hold together. If they find in him their solidity, it is not each one on his own account but in their mutual bond. Christ is their principle of cohesion and harmony; of the created world he makes a cosmos, an ordered universe, giving it a meaning, a value, relating it with an end. He is therefore the dominating centre and like the keystone of the universe.[3]

Thus that narrowness in which the Greeks mortified their love for truth (and thanks to which they spoke of themselves as inexorably opposed to the "barbarians") was shattered by the awareness that all of reality had been redeemed by the action of Christ. *Universality* becomes the essential dimension of the one culture. Nothing could be conceived as foreign to the plan that Christ revealed; in this all things found again their true face, were fully enhanced. "Nihil sine voce."[4]

Christ's light animates the whole universe of human interests and abilities. The light of His presence favours the development of all human "competencies" in all their nuances, as the ever-more precise enhancement of the particular and of the all-embracing dynamism to which it can reawaken human capacity. At the same time it purges these competencies of every frustration and abstraction that would dissolve their integration into an authentic cultural context and destroy the synthesis in which alone they have value.

Thus the attitude that made the Greeks hostile to other cultures and civilizations became a profound capacity to "dialogue": "sift everything, keep what is of value."[5] The union of many voices, when their dissonance and dispersion are submitted to a divine harmony, constitutes finally one single harmony, and the choir, obeying its master, the Logos, does not find its rest and serenity in anything but the Truth itself, when it can say, "Abba, Father"; then, God at once accepts this voice, in complete harmony with the Truth, as the first joy brought Him by His children."[6]

3 In those who have followed Him, Christ has brought about a radical "metanoia," a definitive change of outlook: He has given rise to a radically new sensitivity and judgment.

Christ alone is the beginning of wisdom: only the genuine perpetuation of His presence among us in time, the community of the Church, is the ambit of our "metanoia," the place where Jesus Christ's mentality can become our own.

The community of the Church becomes the matrix of Christian culture.

"*Charitas veritatem parit,*" "Charity is equal to truth." It is a new judgment because it is born of a new life. The new criterion is born of a continually renewed "following," a living faithfulness to the reality of the community, the "death" of any criterion that is "mine." The new culture is born if we accept the rhythm and law of community; and we cannot bring it about in isolation, otherwise we alter the object in the effort. Only a conscious identification with the community's criteria and norms, only an integral dependence on the objective locus of those criteria and directives, in other words, the Authority, is the highway to achieving an authentic Christian culture. Everything must be referred to the community, judged by its measure, grasped with its sensitivity.

So a youth community in the environment educates us in a criterion and sensitivity that generate Christian culture insofar as it *accustoms* people to a systematic revision of the teachings that reach youth, through a continuous comparison of events with the Christian viewpoint.

The term "Christian culture" becomes ambiguous, and more often explicitly void of content, wherever there is only a formal belonging to the Church, and man remains attached to the poverty of his individualism. In this case no Christian culture can be born, the miracle of a wholly Christian personality cannot come about. One is forced to resign oneself to a sad case of "salt that has become insipid," to a "talent hidden underground for fear of losing it"; or many individuals may come forward who resemble those against whom Saint John put the early Christians on their guard, saying, "They are with us but they do not belong to us."[7]

4 *Need for "crisis."* Unfortunately, in our times, the word "crisis" (from the Greek "crino" to sift, judge) is normally understood in a doubtful or negative sense, as if crisis and critique were to coincide automatically with negation; criticism with something that creates scandal, seeking scapegoats and objectionable realities. This is clearly a short-sighted concept of crisis, of critique.

Critique is first of all the expression of our human openness, a keenness intent on discovering being, values. It is enough to add a little sincerity and realistic balance, and the affirmation of those discovered values will clearly imply their limits. The word crisis is not linked to "doubt," but rather to "problem," which in its Greek root means "placing before," setting something before one's eyes.

But what is the *first thing* to place before one's eyes, both chronologically and as a value?

None of us existed; so each of us is formed by a previous fact, a complex of factors that constitutes and shapes him or her. The word "problem" refers first of all to this phenomenon, which is fundamental for a true freshness in the existence of each person and in the life of the human cosmos: *tradition*, the gift with which existence enriches us at birth and in our early development; and the individual, insofar as he or she is aware and intelligent, must sift it and examine it (crìnein). Tradition must "enter a crisis"; it must become a problem. *Crisis* means therefore to become aware of the reality by which we sense our formation. For this reason it requires keenness – not destruction, not intelligence, not pettiness, not a complaint for what is not found, but joy at what is found, and a ready openness to acknowledge the correspondence.

Therefore it is primarily a question of being serious regarding the past; this is the first condition for a mature cultural knowledge of existence and of reality, because there is no culture without a critical approach. Inevitably, this demands taking stock of the tools, structures, and positions with which we will have encounters in life.

To take tradition seriously, to take our own past seriously, means to be engaged with it according to its own essentials, so as to discover its values and to leave behind what is not of value; to discover the correspondence with what we are; and to free ourselves from what could have corresponded only to the situation of other times.

Faithfulness and freedom are thus the two essential conditions for a sense of the past, of history, because history is a permanence that mobilizes itself in ever new versions. And without permanence there would be no freshness, only a continuous frustration with all things. We would have only the fundamental desperation of present-day man's senses: his angry, relentless attempt to resolve all the anxiety of his conscience in a totally different creation. The creation of a totally different human type is a demented frustration, a maniacal myth.

The first great duty of our awareness is to take Christian tradition, the *Church as history*, seriously. This is the most urgent duty of our cultural life, as it will generate our work in the world.

And we need to bring total concentration and openness to this work, a freedom of spirit that will allow us to express our Christianity in a vigorous way, perhaps in innovative ways. And if conditions demand it, we must leave aside the old form with the readiness and flexibility that Jesus spoke of in the Gospel when He said that Christianity and the life He brought is like a wine that is ever new, and you don't put new wine in old skins, nor do you patch an old coat with a new piece of cloth, because then "the tear will get worse"[8]; in other words, the situation will become worse than it was.

NOTES

CHAPTER ONE

1 1 Corinthians 2:4–5.
2 Psalms 54:1.
3 1 Corinthians 10:17.
4 Matthew 5:16.

CHAPTER TWO

1 Genesis 22:1; *see also* Exodus 3.
2 Acts 9:4.
3 *See* Matthew 10; John 20.
4 Acts 9:4.
5 John 17:15, 18, 20–2.
6 John 3:3.
7 John 1:13.

8 John 3:9.

9 *See* Mark 1:27–8, 7:37; John 9:2.

10 Genesis 15:5; Exodus 3:10; Luke 11:28.

11 Psalms 119:2, 49, 92; Psalms 4:7.

12 John 6:68.

13 Matthew 19:29.

14 Psalms 8:5.

15 Exodus 3:11.

16 Jeremiah 1:6.

17 Luke 7:6.

18 Matthew 16:17.

19 Matthew 11:25–7; 13:11.

20 John 14:16–17.

21 John 14:26.

22 John 17:6–7.

23 Romans 8:16.

24 John 15:1–5.

25 John 17:1–3.

26 John 17:26.

27 *The Betrothed*, translation by A. Colquhoun. London: Dent 1968, chapter 23.

28 Mark 9:24.

29 John 16:2–3.

30 Romans 8:9, 26.

31 1 John 1:2.

CHAPTER THREE

1 John 1:3.

2 Romans 6:3–4.

3 Ludwig Hertling, *Geschichte der katholischen Kirch*. Berlin: Morus-Verlag 1949, 36.

4 John 5:39–40.

5 1 Corinthians 1:21.

6 Psalms 119:1, 99.

7 Mark 10:30.

8 Free in the sense of a school guided by educative criteria decided by or accepted by the parents, not those of the state.

9 The writer is speaking of the particular situation in Italy at that time.

10 Matthew 12:36.

11 *Epistle to the Trallians II.*
12 Acts 17:28.

CHAPTER FOUR

1 1 Corinthians 3:23.
2 Galatians 3:28.
3 Matthew 11:21.
4 1 Corinthians 9:22.

CHAPTER FIVE

1 Corinthians 1:23.
2 Clement of Alexandria, *Protrepticus* (*Exhortation to the Greeks*), IX, 88.
3 J. Huby, ed., *Saint Paul: les épitres de la captivité*. Paris: Beauchesne 1947.
4 1 Corinthians 14:11.
5 *See* 1 Thessalonians 5:21.
6 Clement of Alexandria, *Protrepticus* (*Exhortation to the Greeks*), IX, 88.
7 *See* 1 John 2:19.
8 Mark 2:21.

Index